Becoming the Master on the Course and in Life

Becoming the MASTER on the Course and in Life

WISDOM FROM A GOLF PRO AND A MEDITATION MASTER

Geshe YongDong Losar
and Jesse Moussa

Wisdom

Wisdom Publications
132 Perry Street
New York, NY 10014 USA
wisdom.org

Library of Congress Cataloging-in-Publication Data
Names: Losar, Geshe YongDong, 1969– author | Moussa, Jesse author
Title: Becoming the master on the course and in life: wisdom from a golf pro and a meditation master / Geshe YongDong Losar, Jesse Moussa.
Description: First edition. | New York: Wisdom Publications, 2026.
Identifiers: LCCN 2025028732 (print) | LCCN 2025028733 (ebook) | ISBN 9798890700308 paperback | ISBN 9798890700353 ebook
Subjects: LCSH: Meditation—Bon (Tibetan religion) | Golf—Religious aspects. | Bon (Tibetan religion)—Doctrines.
Classification: LCC BQ7982.2 .L67 2026 (print) | LCC BQ7982.2 (ebook) | DDC 299.5/4—dc23/eng/20250915
LC record available at https://lccn.loc.gov/2025028732
LC ebook record available at https://lccn.loc.gov/2025028733

ISBN 979-8-89070-030-8 ebook ISBN 979-8-89070-035-3

30 29 28 27 26 5 4 3 2 1

Cover design by Phil Pascuzzo. Interior design by Gopa & Ted2, Inc.

"Bringing the Mind Home: Letting Go," pages 183–85, was originally published in *Calm Breath, Calm Mind* by Geshe YongDong Losar (Wisdom Publications, 2022).

Printed on acid-free paper that meets the guidelines for permanence and durability of the Production Guidelines for Book Longevity of the Council on Library Resources.
Printed in the United States of America.

MIX
Paper | Supporting responsible forestry
FSC® C005010
FSC www.fsc.org

Contents

Introduction

We first met in 2020, on the golf course: Jesse Moussa the golf pro and YongDong Losar, a *geshe*, the equivalent of a PhD, from Tibet. As we golfed together, we shared our thoughts on life, our values, and our ideas on golf. Through all of our discussions of life journeys and the evolutions of our teaching and learning styles, we started to realize that our thoughts on focus, relaxation, and acceptance resonated with each other. Ideas for teaching golf paralleled ideas for teaching about life and well-being through Tibetan Buddhism. We realized more and more how lessons from one could bring benefits in the other. Our relationship grew through the link in our perspectives on growth, the beauty in life, and the world around us, and especially through our love of golf and the golf course.

Through this connection, we decided to compose a book with parallel writings about the nontangible skills that can take you on a journey to become your own master of golf. Due to the nature of the teachings of the book, it also provides guidance and focus on how to enjoy and grow as a person in your life journey.

The intention of this book is to shift the focus of a game of golf from the score to mindfulness and happiness, to being confident in and knowing who you are. The swing, the ball, and the golf course are all methods to connect to who you are. Trust yourself.

Geshe-la

THE GAME OF golf gives me both pleasure and wisdom.

I love to be on the golf course, enjoying where I am. The fresh air, the water, the bunkers, the trees, and the fairways create an environment that I immensely enjoy. I usually don't take a cart so I can enjoy the walk and be fully aware of this joy in my environment. I am grateful to those who created and maintain the course; I appreciate their time and effort.

I appreciate the physical pleasure of my tiredness after eighteen holes and three or four hours of play. I welcome the mental space I must maintain throughout the game. I must hold on to the wisdom of mindfulness and let go of everything other than being fully present in the moment. When I'm fully present, my club swings free and true. A mishit will clearly demonstrate my lack of mindfulness.

I feel compassion for myself when I become too hard on myself, and I feel the same compassion for other people's feelings as they struggle.

I feel great gratitude for this life. All this wisdom, joy, and pleasure, I wish to give to those who play the game of golf; may this wisdom and joy bring benefit throughout your life.

My intention in this book is that people truly learn that three or four hours on the golf course is an excellent opportunity for spiritual practice. To play golf well you must manage your emotions. We all have stress, trauma, and challenges. Do we run away to the golf course to avoid them? How important is it to deal with these issues internally? Golf doesn't have to be only about the scorecard; instead, it's an excellent opportunity to practice mindfulness, develop wisdom, relax, and take pleasure in our life.

All these skills I've learned and practiced on the golf course. When I leave the course and go home or to work, I practice the virtues I've learned.

We can choose to use the four hours on the course as an opportunity to learn—instead of wasting them—not just how to play golf, but how to be happy, mentally and physically, and have peace and take pleasure in our life. Don't waste this precious moment.

After writing this book and sharing some of its ideas with students, I learned that its concepts apply to all sports. My friend John Coleman, PhD, who is an Olympic coach, stated that the biggest reason for losing is lack of focus and mental strength. My hope is that the psychological support offered in this book will benefit players of any game.

Golf can teach people how to focus both on and off the course; it's great at helping you remember that it's a 99-percent-mental game. There are many books that offer golf techniques and advice, but this book is extraordinary because each chapter focuses on mental and spiritual benefits. You must discover the master within yourself. We don't see the master within, because we don't have the mirror of wisdom, but we can develop this wisdom on the course. Golf can be a method of reflecting your life's journey.

This book is a very special collaboration between Jesse and me. He's a pro golfer who dedicated his whole life to mastering golf; I spent my whole life from age thirteen in spiritual practice. We both love this game, and writing this book together has clarified our purpose on the course. May this book bring great benefit to the reader; may the pleasure of golf help people overcome the struggle of daily life.

Jesse

THIS BOOK HAS great value for all golfers of any level, from those just beginning to develop their skills to those that are highly skilled and are looking for a focus to take them to a new level. Each chapter of this book can be read on its own; each has its own valuable lesson apart from the rest of the book. The book can be read from front to back or via any chapter in any order.

It's not a typical golf book about how to swing a golf club, but rather a compilation of different skills that you can continually practice, mastering your game one golf at a time, and extend that same practice into your daily life, learning to master each moment of your life one at a time. Each chapter or skill provides the opportunity to learn how to balance and center yourself; to focus on the joys of being in the moment; to find fulfillment in the whole game, in every round; to find humility in the triumphs as well as the lows; and to find success in the struggles as well as the wins. The lessons show you how to enjoy the moments with your friends and playing partners—and still focus on the moment to give your best to what you're doing and who you are with. It teaches the power of presence and acceptance in golf and in your daily life, and teaches you how there is a gift to learn and grow in every moment or on every shot, whether from the center of the fairway or behind a formidable oak tree.

I recommend you read the book once through and then pick a topic to focus on and see if you can integrate its lessons while you play or get ready to play a game on the course. It will open your eyes to the habits you mindlessly do that destroy or hinder your best efforts to get better. The more you become aware of these, the more you'll want to make a change, to improve your choices of focus and become disciplined to master your mind.

Give yourself time to play with and learn each lesson and slowly add them to your toolbox of intangible skills that will lead to better golf, a healthier attitude, and inner fulfillment from each golf experience. One day those skills may even seep into your daily living.

Geshe-la's love and reverence for the game of golf beams from his soul on and off the course, and I apply my passion to be the best professional of my sport to every lesson I give, and every round I play. This book is a gift to the students of their art who wish to find their own master within.

1. The Grass

Balancing with your energy
Slowing down with your movement
Grass grows at its own speed
Relaxing with your body
Being clear of your mind

—GESHE-LA

Geshe-la

As I learn the game of golf, one of the most important things I need to keep reminding myself is to slow down: not just my tempo, but my level of urgency and my "trying" dial as well. This same awareness is important in everyday life too. Everyone is on the "go, go, go program," and once they are on it, pushing forward for more of their personal needs or wants, they don't know how to stop. They may even feel guilty if they are not pushing as hard as they can.

I was in Costa Rica when the Covid-19 pandemic started, and everyone was suddenly in lockdown. For many people, this was like an unexpected STOP sign, and I wondered how they would react. So many of us are like ants, working as hard and fast as we can, sometimes forgetting what the original mission was. When we were forced to be still, it led to some stress and, for many people, a wake-up call for healthier change. It is important to take time in our life to be still and balanced, and to find out who we are and have an awareness of what we are doing. True happiness comes when we consciously live and we mindfully do life.

One day Jesse, my golf instructor, told me to slow down and just swing the club without forcing it, and a poem by the Japanese poet Matsuo Basho came to my mind:

> Sitting quietly, doing nothing
> spring comes and the grass grows by itself

If you are just sitting still, everything becomes still. Your mind and thoughts clear. This happens naturally if you don't try to fabricate it or force anything. That is what I practice and teach in life. Grass grows by itself; you don't have to push it to grow. We tend to think that doing nothing is not productive, but it is when you are actively still that you can be most productive and successful. It does not mean you do not work at anything, as we all still need to work and continuously learn; instead, we do it mindfully and with ease and let the productivity show itself in its own time.

The same thing applies to playing golf. You can take lessons, practice, and set goals—then, let your body swing the club. Try to let go of the mind's forceful nature and allow your swing to grow, just as the grass grows; it uses the resources it has at hand and grows in its own time. Some days it is easier to do than others. On days when it is hard to let go and just swing the club or just live the day as it comes, mindfully, just let it go and try again tomorrow. I am here to remind you and myself to slow down; be aware and mindful of what and how you are doing, and good things will grow. When you feel out of sync, as the poem suggests, watch the grass grow.

A friend of mine moved from Hong Kong to northern British Columbia. After a long time, he went back to Hong Kong for a holiday and noticed himself being caught up in the quick pace. But he reminded himself that he was on holiday and didn't have to rush like everyone else, so he slowed down. You have this choice too.

How do we stop always trying to go, go, go? It can be difficult to slow down because of the pace around you.

But it still comes down to a conscious choice. There is a Tibetan saying: "Running, running, you won't catch the others; laughing, laughing, won't satisfy others." It doesn't matter what you do with your body; you must slow your mind down.

Part of my training as a Tibetan monk focuses on mindfulness, really paying attention to what is going on around me and not focusing on stories in my head. Even though our society doesn't seem to always value this, stopping negative thoughts and turning my attention within for a few moments grounds me and opens me to new approaches. This is something I can do in the moment on the golf course.

I can also study and learn more about myself by taking some time to reflect *off* the course. By being curious and without judgment, we can observe a lot about ourselves and make the corrections we need to be happier both on and off the course.

Reflection

When you are in a quiet space and have time to reflect, you may want to consider the following questions:

1. How does the movement of your body affect your mind? Are they tied together, or do they operate separately? What sort of movement brings the best results in your mind?
2. How does your thinking affect your body? If you are stressed, how do you feel? Have you noticed which thoughts bring more calm and positive results in your

body? Which thoughts bring you agitation and more negative results?

3. If you notice that your body and mind are not in balance, how do you balance your body with your mind?

Everyone experiences the same barriers in golf—even Tibetan lamas! I have found that these steps allow me to accomplish what I want: slowing down, being aware of both mind and body, and really observing what is actually happening and then responding without judgment.

We can slow down, focus on the grass, and recognize that it grows naturally at its own pace. We can also be aware of our own mental and physical growth from childhood to now. We all have our own pace of growth that we can recognize and appreciate.

Slowing down can bring quick changes.

Jesse

As a competitive golfer, I can recall so many rounds where the stress and intense drive to have a great round of golf sent me into such a spin that I couldn't find my balance or sense of control. Drive and the determination to be great at something is a positive trait for an athlete, but not when it stifles your ability to perform. Maybe you can remember that feeling at a championship or tournament or maybe while playing golf with your friends or even a boss.

One week, when I was competing on a mini-tour event in the States, I was fortunate to have my wife, Nadine, who is also a professional golfer, caddying for me. She noticed that I had a sense of urgency in my walk and talk before I teed off. She could sense my stress. She said to me, "Honey, stop what you're doing and watch the grass grow—slow your eyes down." At the time I did not appreciate the entirety of what she had said to me, but her words helped me slow down my thoughts and breathe, to play one shot at a time with less panic in the outcome.

We discussed it more after the round. She explained that she used that advice herself whenever she felt out of sorts and stressed on the golf course. When you turn your racing mind away from stressing about swing and score and hazards, and instead focus on something so perfectly green, mowed, and quiet, and try to get so still inside so as to watch it grow, you create a relaxed space in time and in your body. This grounds you, and you can move and think with more relaxation and creativity, instead of reacting to the stress.

Since that day, I have learned to breathe and allow a space inside of me to be clear of stress and distraction, so that I can perform freely. When I play golf, I know I am playing a game that I love. I enjoy being competitive, but often I am able to let go of the intensity, and it feels like I am just on a walk, hitting a golf ball in the direction the land and grass has laid out for me.

I have worked in the golf industry for twenty-plus years and have listened to people talk about their scores every day. They compare their 92 to a great 89, or their 81 to their 79 two days ago. Everyone is trying to better their score, to reach their goal of getting to a new level. Even a regular 70s shooter is focused on breaking 70. These are all great goals, but sometimes we are so caught up in the grind of getting somewhere that we stay stuck in that grind, and it becomes another struggle and stress—and it seems that all our efforts hit a wall. Then it may be time to breathe and watch the grass grow.

Everyone can master the game of golf this way, by remembering to enjoy the process of the game. When you're admiring the beauty of the green laid out in front of you, you won't be fighting the elements of the game or yourself. Your score is the by-product of your walk through a park where nature is beautifully leading you to the hole; your pleasure and presence on the walk create the score.

Your skill level is based on your ability to hit the ball in the direction the hole intends, your ability to trust yourself to do that, and your ability to trust your coach who is helping you improve your natural ability. Even when you are practicing or in a lesson, take a moment to breathe and see the beauty of the moment. Stop the struggle and the push and the grind. Be right there where you are, feeling your club, seeing and feeling the grass, and hearing your instructor. Be open to what is in front of you, and the growth happens within your openness. You cannot force a future result before you make a swing.

Be aware that the grass is a beautiful thing. A game is a walk on something that is prepared perfectly for the ball to roll into the hole, mowed through the trees to show you the way to the green. The mastery of golf has no attachment to the ball or the score. The mastery of golf is acceptance, just as the mastery of yourself is acceptance. I accept the skill level that I have that day. I accept the amount of focus that I'm able to put into the skill. And I accept where the ball goes. Once I have accepted those things the walk becomes light. It's not a struggle to play golf. There's no search for perfection. I'm looking at perfection. Looking at nature. Feeling the wind. Looking at the grass. Listening to the birds. Enjoying the land in front of me as my ball rolls through the grass. The excitement of the display in front of me is more exciting than the score at the end of the day.

There is no doubt that on the golf course the distractions are everywhere: other players, bunkers, houses, out-of-bounds markers, doors banging, people talking, and even your own voice in your head. When I am playing, right before each shot is when I really focus on my target line, and there is no better help with that than looking at the grass in front of the ball. Look to a blade of grass or a leaf or stick gently lying on it that connects your ball to the line to your target. When I take my practice swing, I feel the club brush the grass and I listen to the sound it creates to help me feel the rhythm and timing of my swing. When I line up a putt, I pick a spot on the grass in front of my ball to roll my ball over to get it on the correct line to the hole. The grass on the course is such a big part of each shot you play: Take the time to really look at it and appreciate its color, its texture, the direction in which it grows, and even how long it is. All of this provides your senses with information that helps you with your shot, and tuning in to see these things focuses your creative mind and heightens your sense of space and balance. It creates focus without really trying and disconnects you from the destructive distractions.

I challenge you in your pursuit of your golfing goals to "watch the grass grow"—and *you* will grow, and your game will improve naturally on its own without the extra push and forced pressure that raises adrenaline and panic.

Reflection

What do you do in your game of golf to slow down?

Can you remember a time that you brought a panicky, stressed feeling to a game? Think about how hard it was to play with that energy. For example, do you recall a time when you or your partners complained about a slow round, but when you checked the time, the pace of play was well within the allotted time? So many people mindlessly rush from shot to shot and miss the moments along the way.

The next time you golf, try to focus on the reason you came to play—friends, fresh air, time to relax, or a chance to practice your skills. See if you can notice your running mind and make a conscious choice to slow it down by focusing on something in the present. For instance, on each hole see if you can focus on the rhythm of your footsteps on the grass, the sounds of the birds, the sensation of wind or sun on your skin, or the long grass blowing in the wind—or try to watch the grass grow! You have to really slow down to try to see it. As you play golf, practice focusing on aspects of the grass—the color, texture, or length—even as you wait between shots, and see if it changes your focus.

As the grass grows, so will your focus.

2. Letting Go of Ego and Attachment

When you are standing beside the ball
Even if people are watching, you are alone
Only you and the ball
Only you and the target
Only you and space

Only you and the natural elements surrounding you
Now you are with silence within your head and around you
This is your true master, who you find by yourself
Only then are you ready to act, play, and be

—Geshe-la

Geshe-la

I, SELF, AND *EGO* are different words with the same meaning, and each is a creation of our minds. Identification and preoccupation with ego creates suffering, because the ego sees itself as separate from the rest of the world. This dualistic state of mind creates limitations for ourselves and reduces our connection to others. If we don't understand this separation, we're like insects caught in a spiderweb of attachment, with all the freedom of flying gone.

I have a few stories to tell about ego and attachment. The first two stories tell about the most difficult events in my life.

The most important people in my life are my mother and grandmother (my mother's mother), even though they both passed away when I was young, and so I don't remember much about them. Both were very loving and caring, and they were role models to me.

My mother, whose name was Namgyal Tso, was very gentle and soft. My grandmother, Darkyi Tso, was very gentle and wise, but she could also be very strong. She was a Tibetan medicine practitioner. My mother passed away when I was about five and my grandmother passed away when I was twelve.

When they were gone I felt immense grief. I still feel that way now, when I think of them. The two most important people in my life were gone. I felt I needed to do something for them and make them proud of me. My uncle and other family members were working and business people, and they wanted me to follow in their footsteps. I was only twelve years old, yet I decided to follow a spiritual path. It took my family a long time before they would allow me to do what I felt was best. But I had set my intention to let go of myself and what I wanted in order to benefit and protect my mother and grandmother and make them proud. So eventually I was allowed to become a monk.

Before this decision, I just wanted what I wanted. This was the first time I let go of ego, and this spiritual path continues today. This motivation is my life's commitment.

Later in life I found the adoptive mother who I had always been craving. For seventeen years Amala Norma was my spiritual mother, and then she passed away. The power of grief is still overwhelming when I think of this. We think we grow up and are adults, but I still feel the wound forty-eight years later.

Now I have faced letting go of the three most important ladies in my life. I found it very hard to lose my mother who carried me when pregnant, nurtured me as a small boy, and then was suddenly gone. I learned through this tragedy that when someone is gone you must let go instead of resisting and fighting, which only creates more suffering. I learned more awareness and to have spiritual kindness to myself and others. If I can let go of losing my beloved caregivers, I can let go of anything. I'm glad that as I grew in my spiritual practice I learned more methods and gained more power to handle situations like this in my life.

My second story is about letting go of my homeland.

In 1992, I let go of everything I owned and had built in my twenty-three years of life. This included books, gifts from people in Tibet whom I loved so much, clothes, robes that I wore, the house my uncle built for me, and spiritual items that I had collected from family members, friends, and masters with whom I had special connections. I knew that I might never return to my home, the land where I was born. When I left Tibet, I kept with me only three books of notes that I'd made of my teacher's instructions. There was nothing on my body but robes and clothes and a small backpack. I had to let go of everything else when I left Tibet.

I remember seeing my younger brother, Lhatsam, crying through the bus window as it drove away. I adore Lhatsam in my life and my heart. Although seeing him like that was very difficult, I was eventually able to change that image of him crying, as I knew that his pain was temporary. We spoke after that, and over the years I've been able to see how he's grown up. I still feel fatherly toward him, even though now he's a successful adult

Letting go of attachment is very sensitive. And we're all different: Some people can let go of things quickly; some can take months and years. But it's good to recognize when you see attachment in yourself and others; you can become very sick or even die from hanging on to negative attachment. Letting go is not easy for anybody, but the bottom line is that letting go of attachment and its accompanying suffering can be the best gift to give yourself. This can be the best gift for others as well.

Leaving Tibet, and everything I had in Tibet, over thirty years ago was good for my spiritual journey. Remembering those losses makes it so much easier for me when I have any setbacks or difficulties.

For instance, compare hitting a bad shot on the golf course to losing a loved one or beloved homeland. When someone passes away, that's it, they are gone forever. But a bad shot on the course? I'll have an opportunity to correct it with another shot within the next ten minutes, or at least the next day.

We are all challenged by ego and attachment on a daily basis. We can see it very clearly when we play golf. It's good to learn how to recognize and address it.

We can use every game of golf as an opportunity to let go of attachment and redirect our lives in a more positive direction, away from the ego-driven point of view. We really need to turn our focus away from the "I" to the world outside of ourselves. Instead of focusing on yourself, focus on others. You will find it is the most joyful way to be.

And if you can do it genuinely, truly paying more attention to others' happiness or feelings than to your own ego, your golf game will naturally improve itself. You will play better, because you do not get stuck on focusing on "I." You will enjoy playing more. I have applied this to my game as I do my life practice.

Reflection

Please consider the following questions for both golf and life.

What is your intention before you speak or act? Do you set an intention? What is it? Is your intention for yourself or to benefit others? If your intention is positive, the result can be more positive. A negative intention can create negative results.

What does *ego* mean to you? I notice in the West *ego* can mean "pride," but I see it as a delusional, self-centered view of self that separates us from others. Ego is focussing on yourself without inclusion of others. This can be a limitation that shrinks your own energy and can result in harm to others.

Jesse

THE EGO IS an image or feeling about ourselves that we want to believe and that we try to portray to those around us. We attempt to project this image all the time, and we feel angry or disappointed when we fall short of the idea we have of our best self. I see people operating from their ego-level every day at the golf course, and I know I have been no different for most of my golf experience.

In 2004, I had the opportunity to compete on a developmental golf tour in the United States, thanks to the help and financial support of people willing to afford me this opportunity. For the first few events, I didn't quite make the cut, but at an event in Myrtle Beach, South Carolina, I felt my confidence and comfort level grow, and I played some of my best golf. I had put together two good rounds with a 3 under par total and was watching the leaderboard to see if I had made my first cut. As you can imagine, my ego was excited and proud—I had played solid golf and was feeling like a tour professional. As it turned out though, the scores were low, and I had failed to make the cut. My happy ego then took a hard blow and I had to process the disappointment.

My injured ego was also anticipating the difficult call I had to make to my sponsors explaining the results. I experienced the anxiety of being measured by someone else and being evaluated according to their opinion. As much as I tried to convince them that I was growing and had played good golf, their evaluation of me was that I should be winning the developmental tour events and that my missing the cuts told them I was not good enough to continue. They terminated the sponsorship. My ego bought into the belief of failure and latched onto the focus of missing cuts. I headed back home to Canada with a beaten golf ego, went back to work, and stopped playing golf for months.

As a club professional, I hear people focusing on their longest drive, their best putt, and their birdies to build up their ego. Then there are those who tear themselves down with disappointment because of a badly played round, a failed putt, or a performance worse than a friend's. These players failed to measure up to what their ego wanted them to be, resulting in a constant seesaw of emotions, a feel good / feel bad rollercoaster ride.

We are all in search of ways to feel good about ourselves and the things we do. It is easy to connect with the high of a momentary success and then search for an answer or a possible excuse to explain our failures that lead to anger and disappointment. This is exhausting and does not lead to a consistent level of growth nor a lifelong love of the process.

Over the years of my own golf journey and with my profound relationship with Geshe-la, I have learned a different way to be. We have all heard the saying "Nobody is perfect" and we like to use it when we make mistakes. Rather than using this as an excuse, though, we should instead view the cliché as a rule of reality. This is a very helpful attitude because golf is not a game of perfect shots; the game is a mixed bag of good and bad shots. And sometimes the bad shots work out well, and the good ones are sometimes affected by bad luck. When we watch professional golf on television, we get the impression that these players are so good they hardly ever make mistakes, that they make all of their putts, and that they always shoot under par. We try to reach this unattainable goal when we practice and play. But the reality is you are watching the best players in the world play their best golf on that particular day. Believe me, they have bad days too. What makes them great is that they do not hold on to that bad story. Instead of stewing in their disappointment, they focus on every shot and accept the one that has already been executed. Even after a good shot, they celebrate the enjoyment of it and then let it go and focus on the next one. In this way they allow their emotions to flow without holding on to them. You can learn to do this too.

When you walk in nature and relax to enjoy the experience, it is perfect in itself. You can enjoy the scenery, the sounds of the birds, the feel of the wind, or just the rhythm of your footsteps. This is a great demeanor to bring with you onto the golf course. Try to enjoy the round for the walk and the flow of the energy and allow your score to be secondary to this focus.

You do not need to be focused on your swing or shots all the way around the course. Instead, you should be able to go in and out of focus for each shot and in between enjoy the walk, the green grass, trees, the breeze, sunshine, or the ducks in the pond. This kind of change in focus trains you to let go of each moment and stay in the present, perfect as it is, without attachment to anything before or still to come. This brings a fresh perspective, energy, and clear focus to each shot without it being clouded with emotion or expectations from the past. It takes practice to be self-aware and notice when you are staying attached to an emotion or a shot. It takes practice to focus on the shot, process the result, and then disconnect and focus on the walk and your surroundings again. When you get close to the ball to hit the next shot, start to focus on what you want to achieve and how you are going to achieve it. You will find that you are more in tune with your surroundings; you can feel the elements, like the wind, and see the terrain with more clarity and definition. You can make better decisions on club selection and shot performance with a relaxed mind. This sets a rhythm to the game. When the ego gets entrenched for good or bad, your rhythmic flow gets stuck like a broken record that can't move on.

The ego is attached to something in the past or some desire in the future, which means it is not useful for reality in the present. It is stubborn though and we get addicted to chasing its highs and fighting against its lows. It takes constant practice of self-awareness and choice to focus on the present. That is where your real strength lies—not in your ego. Let the ego go, and get back to enjoying the walk between your shots. Golf is a game of one shot at a time linked together by a rhythmic walk in a park. The shots do not have to be perfect for a great round of golf.

Reflection

Have you ever missed a one-foot putt? How did you feel about that? Even the best in the world miss short putts.

Next time you play or practice, notice your feelings and inner sense of self-worth after you putt, whether the results are good or bad. Take a moment to acknowledge the feeling and process the mistake or success. Then, immediately move your attention to the beauty of nature or the company of friends, and then continue to the next shot with no emotional connection to the previous one. Pay attention to the fresh feeling of a clean slate as you prepare for the next shot. Have fun practicing this process.

3. Playing the Course

I'm Old Man Par.
The path and destination
I present before you.

My friends, the elements,
will challenge your skills.
Be open, accept them as part of our game.

Take time to be present with clear vision.
There is more to enjoy beyond your score.
Acceptance builds strength;
and patience—clarity.

—Jesse

Geshe-la

According to my tradition, the Bon tradition of Tibet, I see Mother Earth as a protective spirit. She consists of the five elements that are the foundation of the universe: earth, water, wind, heat, and space. The earth element is the body of the spirit, the water element is the blood, the wind element is its breath, and the heat element is the fire of the sun. The space element is consciousness, which carries the ball on the course.

When I golf, I see the course as the body of Mother Earth. When I breathe the air on the golf course, I am breathing the breath of the protective spirit. I see the trees and plants on the course as its hair; their roots are its veins. The rivers, ponds, and all the water on the course are the blood of the spirit. Feeling the sunshine, I recognize the heat of the spirit. I respect and feel gratitude to the spirit of each course and to the spirit of the land that was here before the course. I walk very consciously, with appreciation, on each golf course.

It would be nice if every golfer could recognize and acknowledge the spirit of the land before playing, instead of focusing only on the game and whatever fear and anxiety it may produce. Relax and feel appreciation for where you are. We have a great opportunity to develop our own spiritual journey with every step we take. Look around with thoughtfulness and respect the course at a deeper level rather than just as part of a game to be played. Our time spent on the golf course will become much more meaningful.

I am always interested in learning more about golf, and when I have time, I watch it on TV. One day I saw an interview with a golf psychologist. He said that golfers often focus on other golfers or on their scorecard. He said this was a mistake; golfers should just play the course. I felt quite puzzled by this; what did that mean?

The next time I played, I tried to "play the course." As I progressed through my game, I relaxed and realized I was very connected to the course. I looked at each hole and saw the shape of the fairway, the water and other hazards, and the effect of the weather, and I knew where I wanted to hit each shot. I realized how much I enjoy the beautiful and unique qualities of each course. It felt like connecting to the spirit of the land in a very profound way, in the way you can connect very deeply with a friend; you know their history, who they are, and find them easy to be with. Even their day-to-day moods feel comfortable. A course can also change day to day, with pin placement, course grooming, and of course the weather.

Playing the course allowed me to play golf with a deeper understanding and connection to the game and my environment. I had a much better understanding of where to hit and what clubs to use. Sometimes I notice how much more difficult it is to play a new course; I must get to know the course as I would a person. But I can come to understand the spirit of the course by walking it.

The first time I played a course in Jasper, Alberta, a

beautiful town in the Canadian Rockies, I began my usual warm-up routine of hitting balls. Usually, I don't look around too much when warming up; I focus on my swing and stretching. This time my practice shots were going toward a beautiful mountain vista. That day in Jasper, I stopped my warmup because I could only focus on the view. I meditated and connected to the spirit of the land. I felt such joy and excitement and was deeply connected to the land. All my shots that day were peaceful and perfect for me.

When we play against our playing partners or against the scorecard, we do so because we want to compete, and we become very attached to the score. We might think, "How many over par am I?" or "I'm even par. I just have to keep it together for three more holes." Attachment to the scorecard means attachment to expectations and ego—all the things we are working to let go of. Of course, you can keep score, but just write down your number of shots and don't attach any emotion or self-worth to it. When you play with other golfers, there might be days when they play well and other days when you play better. Don't focus on the other person's game; instead think about where you want to play your next shot, what the course is showing you, and how to get the ball to your target.

"Playing the golf course" can be thought of as a method of playing the game. You can start this method at home before you even get to the course or on bad weather days when you cannot play. Close your eyes and visualize the course in your mind. Start on the first tee and see yourself hitting each shot where you want it to go. Have a plan for each hole that matches your level of play, and see it happening for each shot and each hole. Play the course in your mind with your plan and see yourself executing the plan with good rhythm, and focus, and distance control. See each shot landing at your target. It is like playing a perfect practice round, and then when you go to the course, you follow the plan to the best of your ability all the way to the end. This helps you stay focused on how you want to play the course. The scorecard becomes an item in the game and not the judgmental focus. Play the course, not your playing partners, not your expectations, and not the scorecard. Your game will become more consistent, and you will be more confident.

I truly believe that if you don't stay in your head but instead connect to and acknowledge the spirit of the land, it will welcome you. Connect, before just invading this land and walking through it. Before paying attention to the psychologist, I never really understood what a truly spiritual journey there is in connecting to and playing the course. When I remain stuck in my head, I miss so much enjoyment of the game. When I play the course, I connect to the course and set the seed of intention of where the ball should go. If you truly respect the land and its spirit and have a true connection, the spirit of the course will spontaneously support you.

When I connected to the spirit of the land in Jasper, the spirit welcomed me. I still feel joy when I think of this course. The course lifted my energy and everything felt perfect because I connected to the land. There was no negativity in me and I had only positive results.

Reflection

Do you take the time to really see what each course is like?

Do you focus more on competing with other golfers, or the scorecard, instead of playing the course?

Jesse

In my mid-twenties, I trained with my coach and played my golf at Diamond Players Club in Clermont, Florida. I was so comfortable playing that course every day; it felt like I could play it with my eyes closed. I knew the green breaks, the lay of the terrain, and how uphill or downhill holes affected my club choices. On that course, my scores were low and my confidence was high. When I decided to travel and compete on a tour where I would have to play a new golf course every week, I had a big lesson to learn. I felt off balance, unsure, and fatigued from the stress of a constantly changing environment.

There can be risks with being too comfortable with a course as well. When we fall into this routine, we forget to pay attention to the golf course. We hit our routine shots and expect routine results, get pumped about a great shot and complain when our expected shots don't work out. For example, maybe we've successfully hit an eight-iron into the fourth green for the last five times playing, and so without thinking we pull the same club again, expecting the same good result. But on this round, the air might be heavier with humidity, there might be a slight breeze coming over the tree line, or maybe the greenskeeper tucked the pin in the back left corner of the green. Our eight-iron falls ten yards short of our intended target. We start wondering whether we've lost distance, or we blame the maintenance man for the green aprons being too soft or the pin placements too difficult. Some days I hear golfers complaining about the course setup or playing conditions that bother them because it throws them from their mindless routine. The course may not be set up for our best score ever or our natural game. We all want to tee up with the goal of shooting our best round, but maybe that should be redefined as the best round we can play with today's course setup.

I like to refer to the golf course, any course I play, as "Old Man Par"; it is against him that I am ultimately competing. This was a phrase originally coined by the great journalist and golf writer Oscar Keeler, who came up with it while trying to encourage Bobby Jones to play the course, not the opponent.

The course is my friend, and as with your other friends, you should check in and pay attention to their attitude and temperament for that day. A huge part of the game that regular golfers overlook is seeing the course as it reveals itself on every shot. It will be different every day, and the shots required for success will be different every day, whether you are playing your home course or facing a new challenge. A professional player might even change the clubs in their bag to respect a course layout or the weather conditions for a day; they may decide to bring a two-iron instead of a high-flying five-wood to a windy, coastal course. A golfer might decide to leave their driver in the bag if the wind is too strong on a tight hole, in order to find the center of the fairway instead of worrying about distance. The beauty of golf is in seeing and feeling the surroundings, being in tune with your own abilities, and playing the course as it is at that moment.

Be mindful of the playing conditions for the day instead of focusing just on a scoring goal. Sometimes the wind is making the course play longer than usual. Sometimes the holes feel narrow, based on wind direction. Sometimes the water hazard seems more in focus because the ball has an exceptionally bad lie. I advise you to pay attention to the way a hole presents itself and play to the wide space or safe area on the course that day. You can see the wind in the trees or across the water. You can see the slope and lay of the land to the green. You can tell if the ground is hard and fast, or wet and grabbing. Let all of this environmental information guide you in your shot choices, instead of just doing what you always do. When you start doing this diligently for every shot, no matter what golf course, you will empower yourself to play mindful golf. You will realize the same mindful thought-processing and awareness on every shot, no matter where, when, or the type of course condition. It is important to be flexible to match the always-evolving golf course. Being flexible in your mind and shot execution can help you navigate some of the difficult situations and circumstances you may face. Old Man Par gives you a perfect challenge on every shot, but you must see him to appreciate him and perform the shot he is requiring of you. The reality is that to enjoy your game, you need to enjoy the course along the way.

When you play the course and not a score, your golf skills become fluid and truly adaptable. And more importantly, when you pay attention to your beautiful surroundings and absorb the information it is giving you, you become more relaxed and can make better shot choices! Your decisions on shots will be based on smart plays that suit the situation, not a forced or mindless process that only focuses on the end score. You will realize that you can process and play a golf shot on any golf course, on any day, and under any circumstances. Over time you will also notice that your scores start becoming more consistent, and you'll find that a higher score in difficult circumstances or on a more difficult golf course can be just as satisfying as your lowest score in predictable conditions.

Reflection

Have you ever looked at the course as a person? Maybe give them a name, maybe even a different name for every course you play, if you like. They're testing you for eighteen holes, but they also show you everything you need to know; they even offer you measurements to help you. The environmental circumstances are different every day, so try playing each shot and hole with a fresh perspective each time. Think of Old Man Par—or whomever!—as guiding you, instead of tricking you.

4. Focus

Let go of past and future
Being fully connected
No thoughts in the head
Everything is crystal clear and vivid
Perfect and profound with stillness

One thing at a time
Nothing else but seeing the ball clearly
Following the natural swing all the way to finish
Completely open
No thoughts, only awareness
No ego or identity, only one pointed concentration
Fully being oneself without fear

—Geshe-la

Geshe-la

THE FIRST TIME I really learned to focus was one summer in Tibet. I was staying at my master Namkha Tsultrim's house while I studied with another master, Yeshe Gyaltsen. I was the only young monk studying with him that summer; most of the other young monks had gone off with their families to collect medicinal herbs to sell.

I decided to make myself a daily schedule so that I could make the best use of my time, from when I got up at 6:30 a.m. until I went to bed at 9:30 p.m. I scheduled everything: food, meditation, chanting, study time, and calligraphy practice. I just didn't want to waste any time. When I woke up, I immediately threw off my blanket and ran to start the cooking fire and make tea. I then ran back to my room and began my schedule of daily study. I studied, just my teacher and me, and when we met I would run to him and not allow myself to lose focus by stopping and socializing with other monks on the way. I stayed focused and followed that schedule all summer. It was a very enjoyable summer.

That focus led to great progress in my studies. I learned more that summer than I ever had in my life. The next winter, when monks were debating Dharma questions, I did really well and was able to hold my own with higher-level monks. I still reflect fondly on that summer, when I really learned to focus on my life and what I was doing, and the wonderful results it brought.

If we focus on each minute, hour, and day, life becomes very clear.

One summer my golf game became very consistent, which felt really good. My score was most often 70, better than I had done ever before. I reflected on why this had occurred. I noticed that my concentration level was very high, not just on the course but also in my work, exercise, diet, and meditation that year. I focused on what I needed to do each hour, day, and week.

I noticed that I very naturally focused on each shot and was very clear on where I wanted to hit each ball. I saw the ball and the ground and their relationship to one another very clearly. I didn't think of my swing; I just saw the clarity of the ball and where I wanted it to go. When I was clear and relaxed and the ball and the ground were my focus, the swing took care of itself. Without distractions in my mind, my ball went where I wanted it to go.

Since then, when I golf I try to just focus on the ball. When we focus, we succeed, but if we lack focus, there is no success. Sometimes we may even blame something else, like the club or the weather.

Focus is not just for golf but for our whole life. Everything needs focus to be successful: relationships, even spiritual blessings. If someone asks me for a blessing, I focus and trust first. I trust that the mantra or blessing I give has its own energy of blessing. I then focus on the present moment, which has the energy to effect change.

One time after flying to London, I was picked up at the airport by a student who was suffering from a very bad jellyfish sting on his arm. He asked me for healing mantras. I held his arm in mine, and with complete focus, I slowly chanted a healing mantra while blowing its energy onto his skin. This is a traditional Tibetan method of blessing. I immediately saw goosebumps arise on his hand. He said he felt immediate relief. Focus brings the energy that effects change.

Focus is easy to accomplish as long as we're fully in the present moment and not caught up in our thoughts. We need to let go of thoughts and be present in our hearts. If we stay in our heads we're not focused enough, no matter how hard we try.

Focus and *concentration* are two words that are easily and frequently used, but they are not so easy to practice. People often say, "Yeah, you just need to focus" or "I just lost my focus," whenever they are doing something that requires concentration. Deep down, we know that focusing can help us discover and accomplish so many things, but we may not know how to achieve that state purposefully and use it intentionally.

The opposite of focusing is wandering, the wandering of the mind into either the past or the future. The past not only means yesterday or last week or last year; it also means just one second ago. The future doesn't just mean tomorrow or next week or next month or next year; the future can be the next moment, maybe one second from now. To have focus is to be very present in the moment, with all your attention directed right at that very moment.

Most people who are good or talented at something are successful because they can focus, either naturally or through practice. They are focused on the "now," rather than wandering or stuck in the past or future. They are in the moment, that very moment that matters. Anything we accomplish or discover or enjoy is because we are focused on it for that moment in time. When we say "Focus!" we can be too intense or serious. *Focus* does not mean that we are serious and tense. Focus can be completely relaxed.

For golf, concentration and focus are important to playing well. Letting go of the past and not projecting the future allows you to be focused in that moment. Be with the ball. It knows nothing of the past or future. The body has its own memory of your golf swing, but your mind often interrupts that flow, because it's not focused on the present task without interference from frustration with the past or expectation of the future. When you are completely focused with the ball in front of you, then there is nothing else. The focus is completely on the process of the shot at hand, not expectations or fear of results.

When I play golf, it helps if I see nothing but the ball. The ball is very clear. When I'm focused on hitting the ball it is like it is in emptiness or space. The ball goes wherever it goes with no emotional attachment to future result.

For example: When you shoot a target with an arrow, you really focus on the target you want to hit. You are completely focused and can see only that. It's the same when you thread the needle; you focus on the eye of the needle and keep the thread going through. You cannot be thinking of something else and be successful. The task may take only one or two seconds, but however long, you are focused on that singular task. That is how you focus: Be completely present, focus, and concentrate on what you want to effect. Through that concentration, you can hit a target or accomplish whatever you want.

You focus on one moment at a time, and then you focus on one thing at a time. Your senses dial in to the moment. In that moment you are very aware of what you are focused on. When you look at something, be fully engaged and focused only on that one thing that has captured your vision, not on what you hear around you or other unrelated thoughts or feelings. One second, two seconds, one minute, or an hour: When you focus on one thing, one at a time, it makes a big difference for your life and success with your tasks. It is a part of a spiritual practice to liberate our minds as well.

Often our minds are scattered and not focused enough on what we are receiving through each sense. Pay specific attention to what each sense is receiving. What are you seeing, hearing, smelling, touching, and feeling? Focus fully and mindfully on one thing at a time. When we are disconnected from the full experience of our senses and not fully present, we do not experience the joy of the moment. Being fully present is why people can enjoy golf so much and fully appreciate the moment of a beautiful shot.

Awareness and joy come with being fully present and mindful. I remember somebody asked me, "Why do you like golf so much?" It is because I am really focused on the ball, nothing else. I am joyfully focused on the ball in space like a dog playing with a ball. I enjoy this focus, as it gives my mind and body a break from the other thoughts and tasks of daily life.

I forget everything but swinging through the ball—but I do this without attachment to the results of the shot. Attachment is painful. If we are too tightly holding on to something, such as expectations, it can be very difficult to focus. Then we need to shift our mind very purposefully.

One technique I use to shift my mind is to pick five objects to focus on. They may be my breath, as well as what I'm seeing, hearing, touching, and feeling. I focus completely on each sense for a moment and then very consciously switch to the next sense and only engage with that one. I don't get lost in my senses, or overwhelmed, and I manage my experience so that I can be fully present and joyful.

You can, of course, approach the ball with a strategy and apply that strategy, but when the moment comes to take the shot, just focus on that moment. In the moment that you are hitting the ball, your strategy is in place, and you can be completely present and focused on the one simple task of hitting. (Or of painting, or of calculating, or of any task before you.) When you do that, it is simple, good, pure, and beautiful. It feels natural and free of stress.

That is why I think most people enjoy doing things they are good at. They're able to relax into each moment of the process needed to complete the task. They are not wandering or stuck with something else in the past or future that they cannot control. They are focused in the present—and that brings them joy and freedom.

Reflection

If you notice you're really scattered, how do you refocus? What techniques do you use on the course, at work, and at home?

If you like, give this technique a try:

Reflect on what your mind is attached to. Or is your mind scattered? Either way, bring this awareness into your body, almost like retrieving your soul from wandering.

Take a deep breath into your belly. Hold it until you can't anymore. Stay with your breath and feel its energy.

Release the breath and let it go.

Do this three times.

Note that you can still walk down the fairway and focus on your breath at the same time.

Acknowledge what you see around you. Note the grass, trees, water, or people. Mentally acknowledge what you see and stay with each item for at least three seconds.

Then, do the same with each of your other senses: Pay attention to the sounds around you, such as wind, birds, chatter. Acknowledge each and stay with it for three seconds. Do the same with smell. For taste, you can bite a candy and focus on the experience. Notice how you are feeling, and acknowledge your current emotional state.

Your senses can be a door to your inner self. Ensure all five senses are alert, and turn inward. Learn to connect to and release your current experience.

This will really shift your brain and your energy, your balance and your emotional state. How can someone go from laughing to crying? It's because they shift their attention.

When I feel tightness or frustration while playing golf I shift to my five senses and use them to change my energy, like connecting to a bird in flight and freeing myself.

Jesse

I THINK WE all have issues with needing to improve focus and concentration, no matter what task we are doing. Looking back on my golf career I spent a lot of time critiquing my mechanical skills on the course, which admittedly did need some work, but I wish I had taken responsibility earlier in my career to improve my ability to focus. As golfers, we often like to blame a lack of concentration on a shot on others, or something else that caused a distraction, and I was no different.

For instance, one day back when I was competing in an event in Virginia, I was looking forward to a great round of golf with three inspiring golf professionals on a pristine golf course. I began the round calmly and was playing steady golf, but unfortunately one of the gentlemen in my group was not so lucky and was experiencing a tumultuous day. He couldn't find a fairway, quite often couldn't find his ball, needed help with rulings, and lost his composure. This was a grueling day of golf, not only for him but for the whole group. As we progressed, I felt more out of sync with my own rhythm. I was distracted by his game, as I needed to keep his scorecard, and was worried about slow play and the frustrated players behind us. My game, though not quite as bad, was not a success either and I completed that round mentally and physically exhausted.

This tournament led to great discussions about routines and focus with my coach and my now-wife, Nadine.

I realized that I wasn't aware of the importance of having a consistent routine with every shot when I played golf, nor did I know how important that was for my ability to fall into focus and feel a mantra-type rhythm to my game. My head was filled with thoughts about swing mechanics, body feelings, and where I needed the ball to go and how. I asked my coach if, once I mastered my swing mechanics, I would be able to play without thinking.

Now, I have many students that come to me with the same question. Many golfers just want to aim at the target and swing with no thoughts in their head. This sounds wonderfully simple but is not realistic. My instructor taught that it's important to have a swing thought, or feel, to focus on for every shot, to help you concentrate. For me, at the time, it was an intention to make a full backswing, or a bigger turn away from the ball, or to extend to my target on my follow-through. He said it might be a different feel or thought for every round, but that focusing on something was better than nothing at all. I had too many thoughts rambling in my head that lacked clear purpose or organization.

Focus, or *concentrate*, is a verb, which means you are *doing* something with your mind. To be focused means to be holding in your mind a productive thought that will help you achieve your goal, whatever it might be. If we do not give our minds a productive thought or image to focus on, then it is subject to being distracted by absolutely anything—a sound, an obstacle, a thought about tomorrow, or even a water hazard on the right side of the fairway. There is a common saying: "An idle mind is the devil's playground." If your mind is concentrating on the process of what you want to achieve, then there is no room for negative thoughts or distractions. Our mind is constantly on the go, and it is our job to give it a productive focus and train it to stay focused for certain periods of time.

The game of golf takes four to five hours to play. You cannot possibly concentrate for the entire time you are on the course. It is better to learn to go in and out of focus so that you can enjoy your friends and the environment while you are out there.

When most regular golfers play, for the majority of the game they're enjoying the company of their friends, talking about their day and where they don't want to hit their next shot. Then they stand over the ball, and their mind stresses about the wind, the hazard on the left, or the people talking behind them, or they start second-guessing their choice of club. So much is going through their head that they cannot relax. All they can do is hit and hope the balls ends in a reasonably good spot.

On the opposite end of the spectrum, you get the competitive golfer who is playing club championships and wants to compete. They might try to hold their focus for the entire game and, as a result, are exhausted by the end of the day. Neither of these game plans is optimal.

When trying to find answers to my own game, I discovered the importance of a solid, consistent routine when I approach every shot: A routine that has a beginning and an end and specific details that become second nature over time can help turn on focus for the moment its needed and then turn it off in between so that you can relax. To develop a routine that suited me, I started to pay attention to my thoughts and habits when I played and now I even use it on the driving range at the end of my swing mechanics practice.

We all know that when you have a reliable routine in life or at work, things become more relaxed and comfortable and it is easier to focus on the task at hand. When there is no routine, it can feel like random chaos, and you feel like you are getting blown around with no productive direction and cannot concentrate on anything. Having a routine organizes your time and clears your headspace to manage one specific task at a time with clear, focused intention. Having a routine to manage each golf shot does the same thing.

Here is an example of how I play a golf shot: I walk down the fairway to my next shot into the green. On my walk I enjoy talking to my friends and take in the beauty of the air and scenery around me—the birds and trees and the feel of the breeze. As I take in my surroundings and approach my next shot, I look to the trees for information on the wind, I look at the lay of the land to be aware of how it might affect the bounce of the ball, and I become aware of a positive target zone for my next shot. When I'm standing at my ball, I get the yardage to my target, put on my golf glove, and say to myself, "Get your mind right!" This is my trigger to start my focus period. Once I hear this thought, I focus on visualizing the shot and connecting a swing thought that I have for the day with a positive practice swing behind the ball. Then, still standing behind the ball and looking at my target ahead, I align my landing target with a leaf or mark on the ground between the ball and the target, no more than six inches in front of the ball, and I walk into my setup with my clubface aiming at that spot on the ground. Once my body is set up parallel to that target line, I look back to my real target, connect to my swing thought or feeling, and execute the swing. I watch the ball to its ending spot, evaluate my performance, and either acknowledge and learn from any mistakes or celebrate the success of a great shot. I then put my club away and take off my glove and put it in my right back pocket. With this, I am done with that moment of focus. From the moment I say, "Get your mind right" to the point of putting my glove back in my pocket, that is my moment of complete focus on my intended shot. For that period of time, I concentrated completely on the task at hand with a committed focus to completing the shot. Then I enjoy my walk to the next shot and start absorbing information for the next one in a relaxed and present mindset.

I encourage you to pay attention to your mindset when you approach your shots and work on developing a reliable, comfortable routine that becomes your switch to enter your own private space for focus. Once you get used to repeating a routine over every shot, you will notice that your game and your body start to feel the rhythm of the game and it can feel like a dance around the golf course. I prefer to walk the course than to ride a golf cart, as it gives me time to feel grounded and relax, but if you do ride a cart to play, try to be aware of not rushing around from shot to shot; take time to enjoy and absorb the information your surroundings give you and find a routine to begin your focus once you step off the cart. I encourage you to find and practice your focus routine on the driving range, as it will help you align and execute it more consistently, and you can find a routine that is natural to you.

There will be times when a negative thought or a distraction breaks your focus during your routine. It takes discipline to pull out of your setup and start again. You will often see this when you watch the PGA Tour players competing. Sometimes even the best in the world will just continue with their shot even though they were distracted by something, and then they're upset with themselves for not resetting and starting again, as the result is often a poorly executed shot.

The more you practice repeating a focused routine, the better you will get at concentrating on the result you want and the more naturally you will fall into concentration. It does not guarantee a great shot every time—we're human, after all!—but it does improve your chances of creating more successful shots, and it's easier to learn from mistakes when there is a consistent foundation. Let a good shot routine give you the power to focus and become oblivious to distraction.

Reflection

What happens to you when you lose focus? Does your last poor shot continue to distract you from your goal on the next one? Is noise, talking, or slow play a major distraction for you? Think about occurrences on the course that distract your focus and how you react to them. Do you get upset and blame the incident for your bad shot? These are moments of opportunity to get mentally stronger. No course is perfectly quiet for every shot you play.

Practice a routine that helps you turn on your focus when you need it, and if something breaks your focus, see if you can stop your process, acknowledge the disruption calmly, and step back into your routine of focus again. Keep track of your successful focus moments on the course or in practice and build on these successes as you become a master of your concentration.

5. Expectations

Expectation is my own agenda and is not the
nature of universal law
Expectation is a forceful energy and not a joyful
feeling
Expectation is a painful experience when
expectancy is not met
Expectation is an ego state of mind and not the
true natural state of mind
Expectation is a restlessness of being and does
not have the peacefulness of a true journey

—Geshe-la

Geshe-la

IN LATE MARCH 1992, journeying out of Tibet and into India, I passed Mount Everest. I wanted to leave Tibet in order to meet different Buddhist masters, learn English, and see the world and different cultures. I'd had this goal since I was a child; this was the reason I trudged through the snow. We walked through the Himalayas for three days without stopping. We couldn't stop and sleep, because if we fell asleep we would freeze to death. We had not realized how cold it would be and did not have warm enough clothes, and we had no sleeping bags. One monk had one blanket and that was all there was for warmth. Therefore, the only way to survive was to keep walking.

On our third day we were lower in altitude and the snow was behind us. At three o'clock in the morning I suddenly became extremely dizzy and couldn't walk. I wasn't able to speak any more. I felt no pain, but I had no energy left. I thought, "I'm dying now. Too bad I will never meet the masters. I will never see their faces, never learn English, never see the world." I was letting go of everything very quickly and fell unconscious. The altitude sickness, lack of oxygen, and lack of sleep had taken their toll.

Two hours later I woke up. The group had waited for me; they'd covered me with the blanket and held me. I had let go of everything when I fell down, expecting to die, but instead I woke up and was able to finish the journey to India.

Ever since that experience, it is so much easier for me to let go of expectations. It was a very powerful lesson for me. Sometimes it feels like the end of the world when you see your expectations may not be met. But letting go of expectations can bring new life.

Once during a retreat I was hosting on Vancouver Island, a lady asked to speak with me. She began to cry. I could see she was very sad and frustrated, but she was unable to articulate what was going on for her. She decided it was best to leave the retreat.

I wondered what had happened to her. Why was she so sad? Was she not happy with me or the Bon Buddhist teachings? Or maybe her expectations were not being met by the retreat. Sometimes people may attend a retreat with assumptions about the teachings or teacher or even about the food and surroundings. When we have very specific expectations and they're not met, there can be anger or frustration. Sometimes, in these cases, the problem is not with the retreat but with the expectations. This situation can also happen on holidays, when meeting new people, when playing golf, and so on. When our expectations are not met, there can be suffering.

Now when I host retreats, at the beginning I ask people to write down their expectations on a piece of paper. We then burn them so that people may consciously let go of their expectations. Now they are free to accept the food, the weather, the teachings. Letting go of everything allows us to accept everything.

Expectations can be obstacles that block new experiences; letting go of them allows a more relaxed awareness that is open to new opportunities. To the best of our ability, we should be careful of our expectations of others—as well as of ourselves. Holding too tightly to what we want may make us miss everything that is there.

If we could approach everything we do with no expectations about the result, that would be best. But it's hard to stop having any expectations; we all grew up working toward goals and expecting good results from hard work. I approach life with what I call a "50/50" attitude: Maybe what will happen will be favorable, maybe not.

When you prepare to do something, get your mind to accept that there is a 50 percent chance that you might win and 50 percent chance that you might lose. This can apply to getting a job, the success of a business, building relationships, or sports. There is an equal opportunity for good or bad results. If you can prepare your mind clearly with this idea, then you can perform with more peace and feel less pressure. The end result may still be good, but if it's not favorable, you will not feel hurt or disappointed. I practice and teach this 50/50 thought process every day, even with meditation or relaxation. When you settle in with the intention to meditate for a period of time, there is a 50 percent chance that you will have a good meditation session and 50 percent chance that you may be distracted or have a difficult time focusing all the way through. If you have a good meditation, then that's great, but if not, it's okay and you will not be frustrated. You can have good intentions when you do something, and then leave the results up to a 50/50 chance.

In our society, it seems we always have high expectations, especially in sports. We always train for the win and do not teach enough about how to handle the struggle and emotional baggage of losing. We are always expecting to win with hard work. Coaches teach "Win! Win! Win!" But people are not taught to deal with the emotions of losing and failing, which can feel like torture or punishment for not achieving the goal. This is true for the player, the team as a whole, or even a country represented by the team. Sport should be enjoyable. This is more important than winning or losing. Enjoy the process and try not to let the result have an impact on self-worth. Letting go of your expectations is really a key point. If you can do that every day with all that you do, life will be very different.

Reflection

Do you think it is a good idea to have expectations in your life? If you don't meet those expectations, how do you feel? What is the difference between having expectations or not? If you have expectations and meet them, how do you feel? If you have no expectations, how do you feel about the result? What's the difference in your feelings?

Examine your expectations. Sometimes they can be subtle, and you don't notice that they are there. But you will notice if they are met or not. Resentment can be a sign of unmet or unnoticed expectations. Experiment with approaching life with a 50/50 attitude—maybe things will go well, and maybe not. What happens when you approach life this way?

Jesse

WHEN I WAS working hard on my game and competing in professional events in the early 2000s, my expectations were that the longer and harder I practiced, the better I would play. I grew up being taught that hard work begets success, and that learned concept led to expectations. I wanted to be successful at professional golf and was determined to outwork the competition. I believed in the magic of "hard work = success" so much that I was often frustrated when others, who seemed to put in less effort working on their game, would outscore me. The expectations were turning my favorite game into grueling work. They overshadowed my love of what I was doing, and when my shots or scores did not reflect my dedication, the game became a stressful rollercoaster ride of ego-based emotions. When I played well, I felt proud and rewarded, and when I didn't, I would beat myself up emotionally and try to push harder. The more you work at your game, the better you—and others around you—expect you to play. Also, if you have a couple of good rounds, your expectations to continue shooting those numbers or better become more haunting. Expectations are fuel for the ego, which is so easily damaged if you have an off day or week, despite your good efforts.

When I played a course, even when not competing, I would strictly keep score, not only because I was maintaining a handicap, but also to practice beating my last score or to improve my average. One afternoon, when I was playing a casual round of golf with my wife, who was also competing professionally at the time, she told me to replay a shot and try something different. There was no one behind us, and so we started doing this for different shots in our round. It was so much fun and incredibly helpful to our learning process. She shared with me that this was her favorite way to practice—don't keep score, just practice what she had been doing on the driving range on the course, in different situations. We did this often and those rounds of golf became our most valuable practice time—rounds of golf with no expectations, no pressure, but just focused creativity with no limits. I played creatively with no concern for the results. I enjoyed playing every shot for the beauty of that one shot without attachment to the outcome. I remember when I focused on what I expected myself to shoot, I felt tight, controlled, and under pressure, and it became work.

I've learned to enjoy my practice for exactly what it is: practice. And that means trying things I might be scared to do when I play for a score. I do not practice with the expectation of playing a better round tomorrow or next week, but because I just enjoy hitting balls and trying new skills for fun, just like a child plays with a ball or a cardboard box. It's just fun to experiment and see what is possible, and it's a relaxing space to be focused in. I have become aware of my mindset before I practice.

I've learned that I love to practice my golf—and you can too. Try to focus as I do, on the joy of working on improving aspects of your golf swing. I particularly love to spend hours around the chipping green improving my short game. Now, because I value the time I so seldomly get to do these things, I've realized I love to do it just for the sake of doing it. It is amazing how, when you just practice for the sake of enjoying the activity, your skills improve, and you are able to learn and adjust with more clarity. When the mind is relaxed and free of the expectations created by the ego, your brain is free to be creative and learn in a relaxed and enjoyable way.

Now, on the course, I love to hit a golf ball to see what shot I can create, or try what I practiced on the range, for the enjoyment of trying a new skill, instead of worrying about a costly mistake. This practice mindset of no expectations has also given me a different focus in competitive rounds; I just try to create the best shot I can from each situation. In return it has strengthened my confidence. I am not afraid to implement shots like a fade or a draw when needed, because I have practiced them on the course many times before, and I remember the feelings of joy and the rewards of creativity. My mind remembers being relaxed and performing the skills on the course. I feel like I love the game again, and I feel boundless in what I can achieve, because I let go of any scoring expectations.

I have learned that having no expectations for golf, or for life in general, leads to more fun, more possibilities, and more long-term success. The concept of expectations is a difficult one to change, and it takes a lot of discipline and self-awareness, but it is worth the effort.

You can keep a handicap and still set goals for improvement, but practice letting go of having expectations from your efforts. Let the result be whatever it will be. Let your immediate goal be to enjoy the game and the process of learning and playing. Always make sure you are enjoying the process, and the results take care of themselves. Write down some long-term goals and put them away, while you stay focused on your immediate goal. You will reach them sooner than you think and feel fulfilled along the way. Having expectations stifles the enjoyment and often limits the possibilities. I have even taught this to my son in daily life. He sometimes does not want to do an activity because he already has set expectations of what it will be like, but then when he just goes and is open to possibilities, he has a good time. The opposite is true when we do something expecting in our minds to be grandiose and then our ego feels let down when it is different from what we expected. You might have expectations of doing something, but you really have no idea what lies ahead of you. Approach everything with an open mind for limitless possibilities. In a round of golf, a shot that you consider to be less than perfect can sometimes work out better than the one you hit with what you consider to be a perfect swing; and sometimes a tremendous shot can follow a series of poor ones. Practice being open to possibilities—they are limitless—whereas "expectations" set limits and set up failure. It feels more enjoyable to approach golf and life without the boundaries of expectations; just approach each shot or moment for what it has to offer and see what you can do with it. Paint the picture as you go.

Reflection

Does yesterday's golf affect today's golf? Do you say things like "Yesterday I made an 8 on this hole," or "I was out of bounds on this hole the last time I played here"? No two shots are alike, and no two days are either. Tee markers have changed, wind has changed, pin placements have been moved. For practice rounds, try to play the hole differently so that you can see there are many ways to achieve a positive result. For example: A 300-yard hole can be played as a 150-yard shot + 150-yard shot + 2 putts = par 4. You can achieve a positive result from a variety of different circumstances with different tools in your bag. Try not to let your expectations of how you think you should play a hole limit the way you can play it. Practice being creative to be comfortable with change. Try to play without the expectation of a score, but rather with the excitement of limitless possibilities.

6. Relaxation

Relax the mind through the body
Relax the breath through inhalation, and exhalation
Relax the body through balancing the energy
Relax the shoulders and hands through gentleness
Relax the muscles through stillness and grounding

—Geshe-la

Geshe-la

I HAVE LIVED HALF of my life in Asia and half in the West. While in Asia, I was pretty relaxed and my central nervous system was also quite calm and balanced. I believe this was a reflection of the environment I was in. While in Asia I grew up in a small village and then lived in monasteries, which were both very relaxed energetically. I found when my surroundings were relaxed I was relaxed also. Even when I lived within the chaos of India, I was able to maintain my inner calm because of my practice. Some cultures teach how to have peace within chaos.

In 1999 I came to the West and lived in both Europe and North America. When I entered the West, right away my energy and nervous system reacted. For the first time I encountered a culture that was radically different from what I was used to. The language was different, and the people and their energy felt very different as well. My own energy felt out of balance and it was hard to relax. It took a few years to build up my ability to be relaxed and be myself around people. Now I feel comfortable with each person's energy and personality and no longer struggle to be around people from the West.

When I first began teaching Westerners I was conscious of being very stressed and could feel the sweat build under my arms. After a while I realized that it was very difficult to teach people to relax if I wasn't relaxed myself. I consciously made the decision to be relaxed around everyone, particularly my students. Now, prior to meetings I consciously relax and balance my energy. I will chant mantras in order to balance my energy and breath. Everyone who comes to my teachings carries their own energy and personality. And even though everyone is different, they can connect to my energy and be transformed into a more relaxed and receptive state. I notice it is so important to maintain my own balance and connect with everyone. I may not be sure how much people are learning from me, but I learn a great deal by being with them, whether it is with ordinary people, groups, or famous people. My first intention is to always balance my energy and enjoy the experience.

Today I can say that I can be relaxed with anybody, anywhere, whether it's one person or a thousand. One time I was teaching a group of fourteen hundred people in Singapore. I hardly knew anyone, but I was able to set my intention and balance my energy, relax, and teach effectively.

Now I am committed to this practice, particularly when I am feeling stressed or rushed. When I notice stress within me, this is my cue to consciously clear my mind and relax my energy.

Relaxation is a very important part of doing anything, whether for work or enjoyment, including playing golf. Some people stretch before they play golf to help them relax and prepare their bodies so as to prevent injury.

There are also many breathing exercises you can use that are particularly helpful in slowing down the mind and adrenaline running through the body. I have noticed when I golf, if I focus on breathing exercises or meditation, either before I go, or during my game, I do much better. My performance is even better still when I do three weeks of a steady, daily routine practice of breathing and meditation. When I do fifteen to twenty minutes of daily practice, I notice that my brain function changes. My oxygen level, my energy, my balance, and my ability to fully concentrate on my golf, or other activity, all improve.

With our many daily commitments and lack of time we may struggle to commit to routine effort. When we do not keep a routine, our levels of ability, focus, and health go up and down, and our inconsistent efforts do not have as much positive effect. If you want to really affect your brain function and change what you are doing, then you need a steady routine, every day. I would say it takes three weeks to change old habits. This is true for any changes, whether it be learning to relax, mindful breathing, or meditating, or something physical like changing your golf swing. And whatever is happening with your golf swing or your physical body or mental state, it is the brain that is guiding the habit. If you practice mindful breathing, relaxation, and meditation, it will result in changes in all of these areas.

A steady routine of relaxation allows your muscles, your thought processes, and your brain to change. Physically, your muscles will be more relaxed, and you will be able to make changes more effectively. Your mind will be more present, and you will be able to feel an awareness of the body. Your brain will be more able to process thoughts, goals, and outcomes in your life or golf game. When you notice these changes happening, you will see the positive effects and be motivated to keep it going.

I have learned many things from golfing with my friends. I have learned to apply my life practices as a Tibetan monk to my golf game and have found them to be complementary and incredibly helpful. One day when playing golf with my friend Al, I noticed how tight I felt, and I was frustrated with my bad shots. Al suggested I hold the golf club like an egg—firmly enough to not drop it, but not so tight that I break it. I liked the awareness this gave me in my hands and applied this relaxation technique to relax and ground my whole body.

You can use the following technique either on the golf course as you walk down the fairway, before you get out of your car to play, or at home or work. Use it any time to ground and relax yourself for better focus or just to relax in general.

First, start to focus on your feet, feeling any tension in them, and then become aware of the ground underneath them. Feel the ground as you walk, or the warmth or coolness if you are sitting. Be aware of letting the muscles in your feet and calves relax. As you breathe, allow your awareness to move up your legs and into your hips and lower back. Then move your focus into your stomach and diaphragm, feeling the tension drop as you breathe, and let your back and shoulders soften and drop too. As your shoulders relax you will feel the tension in your arms and hands disappear. Feel the weight of your arms hanging beside you. There is a softness and readiness in the body now to allow your mind and body to connect.

I used this meditation technique playing golf and found more flow and power in my swing. I did this every day and found more consistency, which in turn led to more trust and relaxation. I understood what Jesse had been teaching me about softer arms to release the club through the swing with no forced tension.

The same is true of all of life. When you are angry and frustrated or just stressed out and trying too hard to achieve something, remind yourself to relax, take it easy, or be in the moment. There are two states of mind: the ego and the natural. The ego state of mind says "no." When I say "relax," it says "no," because of this and that excuse. The ego always creates a reason to control everything.

The natural state of mind or awareness just says "relax, everything is all right." What matters the most is the moment you are in, because that is all you can affect. When you realize this, you think with more clarity, time seems to slow down, and your mind and muscles move more effectively. Your instincts are sharper when you are relaxed and in the moment.

To succeed is to be peaceful and joyful. Being peaceful and joyful allows you to succeed. If you are a millionaire or a pauper, there can be stress either way. It depends on the state of mind.

The ego is more focused in the head and in the past and future. The natural state, of mind is more focused in the heart and the present moment. Our pets are normally in their natural state, and we can learn a lot from them. A dog or cat is content when fed and feeling safe and relaxed in the moment. They are always in the present and only with stress when feeling threatened in some way. They respond to the threat and then move to the next moment. The teachings, even the general Buddhist teachings, say we should focus more on the natural state of mind, not the ego state of mind. The ego state of mind is what creates all kinds of suffering, problems, and dramas. It's not worth staying focused there as there is no real value to be gained from it.

It is very important to keep reminding yourself to relax. Relax your body, relax your mind, relax your muscles, so that you can stay focused on the present. That is where we have power and creativity. Positive results are created from being relaxed in the moment. The ego is intent on focusing on what was or what might be, but our natural state is focused on right now, which is truly effective.

Reflection

Do you see yourself as a relaxed person? Or just the opposite? On a scale of one to ten where are you? What are your techniques that relax you when you're stressed?

Jesse

PEOPLE PLAY GOLF to relax—a nice walk on green grass with good friends to talk to. However, in reality, things are often more complicated. Often people tend to rush to the course after work or when they have a few hours to escape chores or commitments in other areas of their life. They often arrive for their game stressed about time—or guilty about their "selfish" escape. The golfer runs to the first tee, or if they are lucky, to the range to warm up their bodies with a few swings before they start. I know this because as a club professional I have watched people do it for years. Even with my job, I would run out of the pro shop after a busy day and squeeze in a quick round before I went home. The stressed mind then becomes aware of the tight body, and you play golf frustrated with the way you feel, while you try to make the most of it. You know you are there to enjoy your time, but the ego becomes concerned with what happened in the last round you played: "I played so well last week, I hope my partners do not expect that again!" or "I haven't had a chance to practice, and I don't know these people in my group—I hope I don't slow them down too much." I used to worry that I hadn't had time to practice my game, and maybe I had a tournament happening soon and needed to get some practice time in. Even the player who arrives with positive expectations of their round, maybe because they had a great round yesterday, is still dealing with the stress that expectations can have on your body and mind.

I can remember the first time I actually played a round of golf feeling completely relaxed. It was my first round of golf with my new friend Geshe-la, in the spring of 2020. We had communicated during golf lessons or in the golf shop in passing, but we finally had a chance to play golf together, and I was looking forward to playing with someone that I enjoyed being around so much. Geshe-la is a very relaxed and happy person, who exudes grateful and enthusiastic energy all of the time. He is a wonder and joy to be around; he reminds you of what it is like to see the world through positive, fresh eyes. As you can imagine, it was relaxing right away to meet him on the first tee, because he was excited to play a round of golf and to get to know each other. It was a happy moment with absolutely no judgment. Throughout the round we shared our thoughts and beliefs about the elements, symbols, cultures, and ways to see the golf course. We celebrated each other's good shots, embraced each other's understandings, and enjoyed the game of golf like a spiritual journey in the space of the golf course. I still remember the lightness in my feet, the engagement of my mind with my friend, the game, and the course, and the relaxed, judgment-free mindset I had to everything around me.

After that round, I learned to create that feeling for myself whenever I go to play golf. You see, Geshe-la taught me to strive to be my master in life and on the course. I realized that during that round, it was Geshe-la's presence and wisdom that was so grounding to be around, and it was his complete acceptance that made it safe to feel so relaxed and present in that space. He has taught me that that is the gift that we need to give to ourselves. We can accept ourselves for who we are at all times, remember to connect with the natural world and space that we are engaging with, and enjoy the connection with the people around us and even with our golf ball that we direct around. This way of being takes practice and self-awareness, but I can tell you that it is effective and rewarding.

When we arrive at the golf course wound up tight from the day or stressed about the round to come, we carry with us an attitude about ourselves in that moment. We might be angry, sad, tired, or maybe even happy and confident. Here are some ways that I use to help myself get in a relaxed state to enjoy a better round of golf. Our first job is to recognize how we feel and be okay with that. Don't try to ignore it or fight it; just acknowledge it for what it is. Accepting how we are in that moment brings us to the present and we can be kind and compassionate to ourselves. When we are stressed or in a hurry, we become unaware of our senses and feel detached from our bodies. Many golfers often comment on how they just couldn't feel their swing, or their body felt out of sync or off balance that day, and they had no touch around the greens. These are signs that you are not fully present at that time to enjoy the moment and are not presently engaged to allow your body and mind to be functionally present for the activity at hand.

It's very helpful, either on the way to the course or upon arrival, to take a few minutes to tune in to your senses to bring you back to the moment. Here are some things that

I do when preparing to play: (1) **Smell** the fresh air around me. Breathe in the air and smell the grass and trees. (2) **See** the beauty around me—the trees, mountains, blue sky, smooth-cut greens, and mowed lines in the fairway. (3) **Listen** to the wind in the trees, the birds singing, or the chatter of golfers at the course. (4) Be aware of **taste** in my mouth. I drink some water or chew a candy or gum and become aware of the fresh flavor in my mouth. Then, as I prepare to play, (5) I **feel** the grips on my clubs, the weight of them when I swing, and the tension in my shoulders and hands. In this process I become more aware of myself and body and can focus productively on enjoying my round of golf as my mind and body become present together. These are things that can be done on your way to the course or in just a few minutes while you put your golf shoes on.

If you do have some extra time to warm up before you play, here are some other things that may help to engage the mind and body in productive relaxation and preparation for a round of golf: stretching; shaking out your arms and legs to release tension; slow rhythmic swings on the range to warm up before moving to full speed swing motion; rolling some longer putts (not to a target) on the putting green to feel the speed of the surface; listening to the sound of the ball rolling on the grass; and feeling the rhythm of your steps and the sensation of the ground under your feet. All of these actions help to bring your mind and body to the present and help you to relax in the moment. It's a good idea to remember to tune in to your senses while you play your round too so that you stay engaged in that relaxed state, or so that you can bring yourself back to it if you get distracted by stress or an off-target shot. These tools to engage in the present and to be in tune with your body are all helpful skills that will help you become your own master on the course and in your life, by accepting who you are and how you feel and by engaging in the beauty around you.

Reflection

Before your next round of golf, see if you can find a personal trigger that helps you relax. It can be a song that you like to sing, it might be a memory or a thought of family or a pet, it might be playing with a coin or juggling with a ball, or it could be a simple breathing exercise. Give yourself time to activate this trigger before you play and even during your round if you need it. It can be used as your grounding tool that will make it easier to focus when needed and when enjoying your entire round of golf or practice session. Your trigger may even be engaging your senses as I do, as it makes me feel connected to the wonders of life.

7. Commitment

We are often stuck somewhere or with something
If we fully commit mentally to finish all the way
The universe recognizes it and will support you
Determination can be respected by anyone
Those who are accomplished always look forward
and never look back

—Geshe-la

Geshe-la

When I was quite young, I was asked to make a big commitment; my youngest uncle, Tashi Jamay, asked me to shepherd his sheep. I said yes, and because of this decision, from the ages of nine to twelve, I lived alone as a nomad.

My uncle lived a long way from me. It took over three days by horse to get to his home and it felt like traveling to a different country. Everything was completely new to me: New territory, new people, even the food was different. I grew up in a lower valley in Tibet that was able to grow barley. We made *tsampa*, a kind of porridge, from the barley, and this was what we mostly ate at home. Here in the higher valleys people mostly subsisted off their animals and there was lots of cheese and yogurt.

As a shepherd I didn't live in the village but instead up in the mountains with the six hundred sheep that were under my care. I had no playmates, no other people with me at all. I just rode a yak to follow the sheep through the mountains. It was often difficult and very slippery in winter; as my boots had no tread, I stayed on the yak. My clothes were homemade: My hat was from a fox skin, my jacket was from a sheep, and my shoes were from yak hide. I felt like a caveman all alone in the wilderness.

Winters were extremely cold in that part of Tibet, and it was very difficult sometimes. Sheep need to roam to find grass to eat and will run hard if one of them finds something edible. I had to chase them on my yak and stay with them so a wolf wouldn't kill them. In the spring my job was easier because the sheep would stay in one place and eat the new sprouts of grass.

During these three years I often felt like I wanted to go home. I was lonely, cold, and scared. It was very hard work, but I stayed and fulfilled my commitment.

After three years, my oldest uncle came and took me back home. He said the family had discussed it and it was time for me to return to my own village. My family had wanted to help my youngest uncle because he provided meat for the family, but while they wanted to help him, they felt three years was enough for a boy. I felt good that I kept my commitment. I could have run away, but he was my favorite uncle, so I stayed.

In Tibet at that time private ownership was forbidden and eventually the sheep were turned back over to the Chinese government, although some compensation was received for them. My uncle did well and he was allowed to keep an extra portion, but there was no longer a need for a shepherd.

That was one of the hardest jobs in my life, but I'm glad I fulfilled my commitment to help my youngest uncle. Later, after I had become a monk, this uncle became quite successful and he asked how he could help me. I asked for a house at the monastery, and he built one and gave it to me.

When you commit, how strong is your commitment? What will it take to succeed? Since that time, I've used my sense of commitment to set my intention and accomplish what I need to do.

I have learned that to play golf well, you need

commitment—for instance, commitment to how you're going to swing in order for the ball to go where you want. When I play a round with my fellow players, I find it funny how we all know intellectually what we need to do to swing the club. We all know the correct posture, the correct grip, and we can discuss all the things we have learned from our professional instructor. Then, the moment we start to take the club into a backswing on the course, it's as if we forget it all. For me, one of the hardest things to do is to slow down my mind and effort when I swing. In my pre-shot routine I say to myself, "I am committed to reducing my forced effort. Don't kill the ball, just swing naturally and let gravity accelerate the club." And I am sure you are familiar with what happens as I reach the top of my backswing—I forget my commitment and I can hear my mind urging me to swing faster, hit it stronger, and make the ball go further. The result of this non-commitment is a poor shot.

The hardest part about being committed to something is not the decision to commit but the follow-through. In golf you get to practice this on every single shot. I have to practice swinging past the ball, all the way to the end of my follow-through, without forcing extra speed, and just letting the club flow naturally to the very end, with good balance. My commitment is not complete until after the ball has gone. If you do not follow your commitment to the end, then the action does not succeed.

According to my Buddhist tradition, commitment is the most important aspect on your spiritual journey. When you are committed within yourself completely to an action, the universe knows that you are 100 percent involved and there are no obstacles in your way to succeed. If there is no commitment made or the commitment is not strong enough, then obstacles will be in your path to show you that you need to be stronger or more sure of what you are doing.

This is an important concept to master no matter what you are doing in your life, whether playing golf, meditating, building relationships, or doing anything you want to do successfully. If your commitment is strong and steady to the end, you will succeed.

Reflection

Are you a person who commits? Or do you constantly change? What do you see as commitment, and how does that impact your life?

Jesse

COMMITMENT seems to be such a big, scary word in our lives. We are selective about what we commit ourselves to. Sometimes this is because we're unsure if it's something we want to do or we're worried about how much work it will be. Other times it may be because we're aware of the difficulty of sticking to something when it gets tough or uncomfortable; no one likes to feel like they have failed. Yet even in golf, commitment is necessary for success.

Lots of people choose to play golf for fun, and their level of commitment is just to their friends and the tee time, which is great. I think we all need this kind of activity. But then there are those who get hooked by the game and want to improve their skills. These golfers are great at committing time and energy to practicing and educating themselves on how to improve. When I listen to discussions in the pro shop or when golfers come to talk to me after their rounds, I notice that the breakdown in commitment happens on their walk to the first tee and over the ball when they start their swing.

People often ask me, "Why can I make the changes to my swing on the range and hit the ball great, but I can't repeat it during a round on the golf course?" On the range there are no consequences to an errant shot, so you feel free to experiment with new thoughts and moves and to swing freely. When you head to the first tee, however, your mind starts to focus on the score and the expectation of playing well. When you stand on the first tee, your mind changes focus to that darn tree on the right side of the fairway or the out-of-bounds on the left. Your body reacts to the mind's awareness by trying to control the ball straight down the middle, out of fear of missing a shot. Where did your clear-swing thoughts from the practice range go? You stand over the ball ready to hit the shot, a little tight because you don't want to mishit it, and half thinking of the swing thoughts you had on the range. Many believe they are not supposed to be having any swing thoughts at all when they play and should just swing. Does that sound like commitment to you? It sounds like confusion, apprehension, and absent-mindedness to me.

Back in the early 2000s, I used to play some local professional Monday games at Forest Lake Golf Club in Apopka, Florida, and for some extra fun, I used to play a putting game on the practice green with one of the guys. He would beat me regularly, and once I had learned my lesson by losing my money too often, I realized that I kept missing putts on the same side of the hole. It dawned on me that I had an alignment problem. I could read the greens well, but when I stood over the putt, I would misalign the putter. This often happens with golfers where their eye line over the ball doesn't match where they want to go. I had to make a change to get better. I decided to literally draw a line on my ball and use it to point my ball at the chosen target line during my setup. Then I would address the ball by matching my putter to the line on my ball. If you have ever tried this, you may know that when you first start doing it, and you stand over the ball ready to putt, the line does not look like it is pointing at the correct line, but when you look at it from behind the ball, it looks correct. I had to learn to trust the line and my setup, and just make a good stroke down the target line as indicated on my ball.

This was the beginning of my journey to truly understanding commitment to a shot. Once I had my ball perfectly aligned to my chosen target line for the putt, I had to address the ball and stroke down the line I had chosen, without questioning the idea that it looked incorrect. The more I trusted my read and the line on my ball, the better my putting got, and the more relaxed I became. Once I addressed the ball by matching that line, it was like I was standing in a box and all I needed to focus on was making a good stroke through that line in my box—and accepting that the result after I performed the stroke was out of my control. I learned that once I was in that space, I made a complete commitment to that line, and my job was to execute the stroke with confidence and be okay with the result.

In comparison, in the past I would pick my target line according to my read on the green and then make a stroke down that line, but I didn't really have a process to rely on and would often second-guess myself or try to manipulate the ball into the hole. As I mentioned, I also had an alignment problem, which led to an inconsistent stroke, inconsistent results, and unreliable confidence. Once I trained myself to trust the line on the ball, I became committed to that line and that process over every putt. I still do this today, and my putting is my best skill and the most relaxed part of my game. I have since expanded the idea to the rest of my game. Once I have addressed the ball, I am in the committed space to execute my swing to the best of my ability, without doubt of the outcome, and then accept and learn from the result after the completion of the execution. This is commitment in the moment, one shot at a time.

You can use this same process if you are making a swing change and want to stay committed to that feeling or thought that was working on the range and bring it to the course. A shot is a shot whether on the course or on the range; the action required is no different, so why would you respond differently to it just because the scenery looks different? Every shot has a beginning and an end. Once you set up to your address position, in the direction you want to hit the ball, you are in your focus or execution box—focus on the motion you want to make, and that's it. Even the great players on tour will have a feel or thought that they commit to. To be focused on the golf course you need to give your mind something constructive as a focal point or it will wander in directions you do not wish it to go.

The first commitment is to take what you were working on with you to the course. The second part of the commitment is to stay calmly focused through the completion of the swing. Sometimes players have the correct intention over the ball and then as they reach the top of their backswing, adrenaline, apprehension, and desire kick in, and they rush down into the ball to hit it as hard as they can or strike with a hit-and-hope mentality. This is because your mind jumps to trying to force a result before you have finished the process. This second part of commitment takes self-awareness, discipline, and practice. I assure you, though, that you will get better over time, the more you become aware of your mindset.

Decide before you hit the ball what your focus thought, or feel, is. Practice swings are useful for this. When you walk in to address the ball, be aware of completing the whole swing with this intended focus. When you do this, it feels like time slows down, and it feels like you have all day to swing. There is no rush, just quiet focus on your intended feel or thought. The result will be what it will be, and you will get great feedback from the result if you have completely committed to the concept you were trying to practice. If you haphazardly hit the ball with a bit of focus on your swing thought, a bit of focus on hazards and targets, and some intention on trying to hit the ball, then the result has no good information for you to draw from, as the method and intention were unclear.

The old adage of "one shot at a time" is true because it is built on the foundation of commitment to a thought, or a moment, to completion. Your score is the total of all these completed focus moments. You will find that the more swings you make with clear commitment to a thought or feel, the lower your scores will become. And eventually there will be days when your swing changes start feeling more natural and your focus thoughts can change more to connecting with targets, and then you will really start to see big improvements. If you are making swing improvements, commit to the change completely, and you will reap the rewards later. Any commitment to improvement is never without struggle, but that is why it feels so rewarding when you start to reap the benefits of your work.

Reflection

Do you have a call to action when you play? A constructive thought or focus for every shot? After I do my best to commit to my shot, I give up all responsibility for the outcome. Bad and good bounces are a part of the game, and the hazards, trees, or bunkers are only distractions. There may be more distractions on the course than on the range, but the shot is the same. You still have to commit to a swing motion for the ball to fly toward the target.

On your next round of golf, see how often you can commit to each shot. How often did you have complete focus on the intended motion, till the end, and give up responsibility for the outcome? I know that the more I commit to and conquer my swing changes, the better the results will ultimately become. When you are making swing changes or have a swing feel to hit better shots, give up responsibility for the outcome and just commit to the swing process you are trying to make. Just like you do on the range. There are great rewards to strong commitment.

8. Life and Golf

Golf can be a mirror to reflect our daily lives
Golf reminds us how to deal with our internal emotion
Golf can be a spiritual journey to find inner peace and develop kindness
Golf can be a game of enjoyment and freedom from stress
Golf can be a time of reflecting on ourselves and connecting with others
Golf can be a method of learning mindfulness and kindness toward oneself and others

—Geshe-la

Geshe-la

When I was a child I had only one toy that I remember: a badminton racket that my uncle Choe Choe bought as a gift for me. I used it to play badminton with the other children of my village. I enjoyed it very much.

Between the ages of seven and nine, I attended our village school. There, I had a chance to learn and play basketball with the other children. It was a lot of fun.

Between the ages of nine and twelve, I was a nomad, shepherding sheep in the mountains. I was completely alone with the sheep. I had no toys with me, no school, and no other children to play with. There was really nothing around me to support a game. Instead, watching ants became a game for me. I used to turn over rocks and watch the ants beneath respond to this change. They would scurry about and move their eggs into a safer position. I would then move on to another rock and do the same. This was my entertainment. But I had no physical games.

Later when I was studying in the monastery, there were no organized sports. But when I carried water from the well with the other young monks, we used to imagine that the pole used to hold the buckets was a kung fu weapon. We couldn't spend too much time playing, but we enjoyed the few moments we had. Because there were no games in the monastery, my imaginary kung fu stick was my only toy for eleven and a half years. Occasionally I was able to run into town with a few other young monks to find a pickup game of basketball. I really enjoyed playing and enhancing my skills at shooting and defense. I believe it is very important for children to have toys that encourage movement; I wish young monks had some time built into their curriculum for sport and exercise.

After leaving Tibet, when I lived in Nepal and India, I was able to watch football (soccer) on TV. Everywhere I went TVs were tuned to a match and everyone seemed to be very into it. Tibetan schools and villages had their own teams, which were closely followed.

In India it seemed that if a TV wasn't tuned to football, it was tuned to cricket. I didn't understand the rules or system of the game, but I watched them throw and hit a ball.

When I came to Canada, I met a husband and wife who played golf. They took me to my first golf course. We started off by practicing putting. As I got used to hitting the small white ball, I thought, "I can do this." I saw it was a game about using your natural balance, your sense of measurement, and the swing of the club. I figured out that it was about the weight of the swing and the line to the hole.

Then I played my first nine holes. Most of my shots were what you might expect: pretty bad. But on one hole I teed up one hundred and fifty yards from the pin. There were two trees in front of me. I decided to hit the ball between them. I hit the ball, and it went exactly where I wanted, between the trees and onto the green. I wasn't sure how close I was to the pin, but I was so excited! I told myself, I am going to play this game. That one shot made me commit to golf.

The whole world plays sports. It can be a big part of someone's life and sense of connectedness. A whole country will be joyful in victory and mourn together in loss. Some people connect to sport so much they may feel "no winning, no life."

I notice many sports involve tirelessly chasing a ball. It can be large or small or of different shapes, like a football or baseball, tennis ball or golf ball. We are humans, but we can be like a dog with a ball, completely present and having lots of fun.

Golf comes down to understanding the system and hitting the ball. This game has become very special to me; it allows me to see my mind. If your lifestyle, work life, relationships, health, and brain function are not balanced, it will affect your golf game. If you are practicing a mindful tradition, playing golf can be an important part of your life's journey. Golf can help the rest of your life become more balanced.

I've noticed that remaining present and willingly accepting whatever the game presents to us is very good practice for life, because the ability to do this improves our life's journey. The challenges on the golf course are often the same as in the rest of our life. I need to focus my wandering mind and be aware of and control unhelpful emotional reactions. On the course we can find out who we are.

One time I was playing with Akarpa, a monk friend of mine, and he told me that I am like a different person on the course; my joy was so clear and obvious. I actually feel that I am more myself on the golf course than in any other place. I'm just present, hitting and following the ball. I see the beautiful nature that surrounds me, and golf and life are together, not separate. I just need to be willing to hit and follow the ball. I try to express this same openness and joy wherever I am and whoever I am with.

So golf and life are very much the same. If you know how to play golf, you know how to live your life. My wish and my goal is for all people to take the opportunity to play golf with mindfulness and gratitude, and use it to improve their lifestyle and health. With golf we can practice kindness to ourselves and others, along with the wisdom of letting go. All chapters in this book provide the reader with methods to improve not just their golf game but their life. There is no separation between the two.

After I began playing golf, I came to the realization that the game often evokes the same internal reactions and feelings as experienced in everyday life outside the golf course. I know golfers can agree with me that when you hit an errant shot, it can be horribly disappointing or frustrating. Especially when you have a good round going and then it starts to go sideways. The same emotions arise in the rest of life as well, whether because of business dealings or partnerships that are getting complicated or frustrating, or because a deal is not going as planned. Global or local news can trigger reactions in our minds, as do small events that happen in our regular day, like getting poor service or the car breaking down when you are running late. It would be amazing if you could learn to handle any situation in your day, whether it be in general life or during your round of golf, with integrity, dignity, loving kindness, and peace.

I have seen people start their round well and happy, but if they start hitting bad shots or missing putts, they don't handle their emotions very well. They may start to drink or smoke to help them cope, or to suppress their feelings. They think this behavior will help them, but in many cases the emotions just become harder to control. People often react to emotional strain in their daily lives with the same ineffective habits and frustrated turmoil. They live in their own emotional mind too much.

I think that golf is the perfect avenue to practice dealing with emotions in a healthier way. Is it easy? No, but it is possible. I will share with you my approach to this challenge, which is a daily practice for me. I find it easier to handle my emotional stress on days when I consciously prepare to let go of my own emotions and instead focus on the beauty of nature around me. If I focus more on the fresh air, and the nice people I am playing with, and less on my score in the game, then I have a healthier emotional day and often my round of golf is better than it would have been if I got wrapped up in my own emotional rollercoaster ride.

I try to approach life the same way.

Always consciously choose to focus on those outside of yourself and the peace of beautiful nature around you. Good and bad things will still happen in the day or on the golf course, but if you do not attach yourself so much to your own internal emotions, you will find it easier to let go of the struggle and move forward with healthier peace and clarity. If you can use this practice on the golf course, it will help you in life. I see it with myself whenever I play a game. I think golf is a great practice ground for life.

Reflection

What is your innermost intention when you play golf? Before I start playing golf, I consider what I am thinking and feeling.

What have you learned from golf that has improved your lifestyle? Or is your lifestyle getting worse? If your life is balanced, how does it affect your golf game?

Jesse

IT'S AMAZING how both life and golf often reflect on one another. Golf, and sports in general, tests your skills, your ego, your tenacity, your ability to deal with triumph and failure. Golf can bring great happiness and in the next shot display your faults. Golf is a game, and there is always another shot, another round, or another tournament to try again and keep learning. In life, there is another day or another circumstance to try to do better next time based on what we have learned. But there is only one life to live, and we all want to live it with as much appreciation, happiness, and well-being as we can. We know time is precious. Life is a journey and as we face our challenges and celebrate our successes, we hope to learn and grow with every experience we face. Golf can be seen in the same way, and players may benefit from thinking of it with more of a long-term perspective, just as we do with life.

Golf can teach us a lot about ourselves and those around us. It has a way of uncovering personality traits, especially the way we face challenges. It can highlight what you are attached to and what you are willing to let go of. Some people, for example, will keep looking for a lost ball for as long as they can, rather than taking a penalty shot. Others will let it go and move on much quicker. Sometimes you will see a player continuously hit the same bad shot and get very angry—but they will not try to think of another way to perform it, nor try to find the error and make a change. You can see this in life sometimes too, such as when a friend keeps repeating the same mistake or always approaches an issue with the same attitude or rigid perspective. In life and in golf, we will keep banging our heads in frustration until we realize that we can approach things with a new perspective: We can try to get more information or use different tools to see if we get a better result.

My golf journey really picked up pace when I met my wife, Nadine. She was a golf professional too, so the two of us got to know each other while we supported each other in our golf careers. One of the personality traits of mine that Nadine got to witness was my constant need to push forward in the world. For instance, I put a lot of pressure on myself to get things done quickly. Nadine noticed how this trait, although sometimes efficient in life, was hurting my game. I would put pressure on shots to be made to try to force birdies and then blow a good round with bogeys or doubles coming in. It has taken some time for me to learn that every shot to the end should be played according to its own requirements, without some justification to a fictitious future result. I have learned to stay present, to focus 100 percent on the shot at hand, and to not project my thoughts into what the field's score might be at the end of the day. Most of the time now, I finish my round feeling like I played it to the best of my ability, with smart decision making, and my final score often fares well in the tournament results. Every now and then I still get caught trying to force a birdie on the holes coming home and make a double bogey instead—and then realize that a par would have finished me in a much stronger position.

This dynamic is of course at play for me in the rest of life, too. In many jobs I have pushed forward to create change for success, only to end up frustrating those around me. Change is often difficult for some and can result in more challenges that require attention. I am comfortable with change and discomfort and feel a need to keep driving things forward. It can be a strong trait, and in other cases it can be inappropriate or not needed. Sometimes your greatest strength can be your greatest weakness. Over the years, I have become very aware that how I live or perceive my life is definitely reflected in my golf game. I have also realized that skills that I have learned to use on the golf course, like patience, concentration, and being present, can be transferred to my life and work.

My breakthrough in life and in my game of golf came when I started to accept with love and appreciation all that came my way—the good, the bad, and the ugly. I accepted my faults, the traumas and challenges, and my triumphs and my joys as all a perfect part of my growth in life. I started seeing that the same attitude on the golf course resulted in better scores and that I had greater clarity on my weaknesses that needed work. It is a kinder and more productive approach. I accept the wind, the trees, the lie of my golf ball, and my injuries and talents as gifts and tools to help me learn. I enjoy the walk and all that it shows me along the way. I noticed that when I react with acceptance on the golf course, I can see my triumphs more, and in life, people start to notice my faults less and celebrate my triumphs with me, because my own energy has a healthier focus.

Almost all the students I meet say they play golf for fun, and yet I see frustration, stress, and expectations that lead to beaten egos every day. Just as in life when we have expectations about how life is "supposed to be," and we worry about how we do not measure up to our own expectations or those of others around us, the same is true for golf. Players might worry about what they look like to others around them, or how they're wasting their time if they're not improving as fast as they'd like. We let our egos control our emotions and actions.

When you play a round of golf or are working on your skills on the practice range, see if you can notice, almost like an outsider, some personality traits or dynamics that affect what you are doing. If you have a close friend or family member that plays golf, one who knows you very well and who you know very well, a game together can be an opportunity to learn together. Remember to be kind and gentle in this process. Maybe, for example, you get frustrated with yourself quickly. Take a look at your daily life and see if you are the same way with other things you do, or maybe it's stress from your life that you are bringing to your golf game. It is amazing what a gift it is to have an awareness of a pattern and acknowledge the trait. This awakening can be a "eureka" moment because it is an opportunity to create change and development both in life and your golf game.

Life is a journey, with opportunities to learn and people to discover things with. So is the game of golf. There is only one life to live, though, and golf is a game within that journey, and it offers an opportunity to see and grow such amazing skills. It is a valuable gift to enjoy the path you are on and enjoy the learning process in all that you are doing.

Reflection

Do you let your golf game change the way you behave? Do you lose control of your temper or lose self-confidence when things don't go well?

Next time you play, when you perform a shot that upsets you or you start to lose control due to failure at something, take control of the situation by making a note on your scorecard as to what happened in that moment. You can reflect on these moments after the round. If it is a reaction you link to other events in your life, it can be a learning moment to try to create a change. If it is a mechanical golf skill that you notice needs extra work, you can choose to get instruction help or dedicate more time to work on it.

By making a note, you change your perspective to third person; now, you're looking in on your game and yourself with a little more distance to help improve things from a new perspective. It is empowering to have self-awareness and take personal responsibility to make a change. Over the next couple of weeks see if you can notice how you bring life lessons to golf or how you might bring some golf skills to your life, even if it's something as simple as remembering to breathe in the fresh air.

9. Mindfulness

Remember you are breathing when you are lost
in thought

Remember where you are

Remember you are here to see the ball with your
heart

Remember you can see the nature of the five
elements around you

Remember you are connected to everything
around you

Golfing with clear awareness brings everything
together

—Geshe-la

Geshe-la

WHEN I WAS seven years old, my grandmother Darkyi taught me to reflect on my day's events and activities every night before I went to sleep. Through this practice, I gained an understanding of how to be present with and feel gratitude for what I had done and any positive occurrences that had happened. For negative incidents, I was taught to let them go and recognize that I should not behave that way again. In addition, I was instructed to dedicate good deeds to those who showed kindness to me; my parents, uncles, aunties, and grandmother were the usual recipients of these dedications. I would recite the compassion mantra, OM MA TRI MU YE SA LE DU, for their well-being every night before I slept. Grandmother Darkyi instructed me that every day I must say Tibetan prayers while being mindful of the past, present, and future. I learned to be careful to use the mantras properly and to share their good energy with others. This was my first introduction to mindfulness.

Later, when I was studying in the monastery, one morning when I was making tea, my master, Namkha Tsultrim, taught me about mindfulness. He asked me to expand my awareness from what was in front of me and to consider who grew the tea and the many people involved in processing it and transporting it to our kitchen. I learned it was important to be aware of and feel gratitude for the effort people put into bringing us this tea. Now, when I drink tea I dip my ring finger in and flick an offering of tea to the protectors and the three jewels: the Sangye (enlightened beings), Bon (the noble teachings), and Shenrab (the community). I also always remember that, as a sign of respect, two hands should always be used in offering a cup of tea.

These two small lessons, of being mindful of serving and drinking tea and of practicing mindfulness before going to bed, have impacted my life every day since I learned them from my grandmother and master. I am so grateful to them both. I know this is not an intellectual or philosophical approach to mindfulness; instead, it is how to live every moment of every day.

In 1992, when I was twenty-three years old, I did a very intensive mindfulness practice. That year I worked on my *ngondro*, or preliminary practice, with the guidance and blessing of my teacher Jawob Rinpoche. This spiritual journey required chanting nine different mantras one hundred thousand times each, along with accompanying prostrations and mandala offerings. When I first began prostrating, it was very painful as my body wasn't used to this full-torso repetitive movement. My body was in such pain it was difficult to sleep the first two or three weeks. But gradually I began to experience intense bliss and joy as the practice took over. I had wanted to go deeper in my practice, and the key learning I received was more mindfulness on an intense spiritual level.

When I came to the West, I learned that in playing golf one must be mindful in order to hit the ball.

What does *mindfulness* mean? Literally, there are two

parts to this word: "mind" and "fullness." "Mind," here, is your internal consciousness, and "fullness" means not half or partial, but full or complete. Our mind is often not fully focused on one thing but divided between several things. When we look at something through our eyes, at the same time we might hear something through our ears, or smell something else through our nose, or think about something else with our mind, or taste something else with the tongue. All our senses—in Buddhism, the mind is considered to be one of the sense organs—are working at the same time and often pick up on different things, so that they can distract from what we originally focused on with our eyes. One way of practicing being mindful is to focus fully with one of the senses on something. When you can see something in its entirety, not half or part of it, that is one way of being mindful. Another way to understand mindfulness is to notice how often we are half in the past or in the future, not in the present, not fully in this moment. Then the mind is not fully present, and we are not being truly mindful.

In Tibetan, mindfulness is called *drenpa*, which means "remember": remembering to be present, in the moment. There are many ways we can practice, including while playing golf or any other sport.

Often, in our everyday life, our minds are stuck or wandering in the past or future. We are not fully in the present. When we come to the golf course, our mind might not be fully there in the clubhouse, with the pros or workers or players that are there. You may still be thinking about the stress at work or about the round of golf ahead. When you check in and are ready to play golf, be mindful of the people who you are talking to at the clubhouse. Be fully present with them, notice how they are doing, and acknowledge their presence there with you. Be aware of your focus. When you play the course, don't just focus on what score you are going to get or want to get. Instead, be grateful for the course; be mindful that you are grateful to be able to play golf at this course on this day. You can say to yourself, "I recognize that this golf course did not just happen or appear suddenly. It took days, weeks, months, and years of work and care to build so that it is here for me to play today." Also, be aware of the many people working to take care of the course and how many people worked to design it.

Recognizing and acknowledging the energy and focus required to prepare the course for you to play is a way to be mindful. Pay attention to anyone walking with you—who are they and how are they doing? Be mindful or thoughtful of the ball, seeing it completely instead of being stuck on thoughts of the result you expect, with anxiety about a similar shot in the past, or fear of what someone else might think. Remember to be fully present with the ball while holding the golf club. When you are not hitting a shot, look at the people around you deeply from your heart, with eyes from your heart. See all the trees, water, air, sun, and beauty of everything around you. Remember to be present with what is around you and in front of you instead of focusing on the score, hurrying through to get done by a certain time, or thinking about work you need to get done tomorrow.

Be mindful of the other players: their feelings, their wishes, their goals. They are the same as your own feelings and wishes. Pay attention to them. Remember to consider what their feelings are. That is a mindfulness practice and an opportunity to really learn internally. It is a part of your journey to learn about yourself through golf with others. It is an opportunity to practice being mindful of everything around and within you, through internal awareness and mindfulness of your attention, thoughts, and behaviors.

When you play golf, take the opportunity to be mindful all the way from your toes, your feet, all the way up through your legs, stomach, and hands, your balance, the way you hold the club, what you are feeling and thinking. Be aware of any tightness, nervousness, or thoughts. Be present before you swing or hit the ball. Be mindful of where and how you swing, without thinking about the future or the past.

There is also mindfulness of the senses. Be mindful of what you see and hear around you. Listen to the birds singing, and the sound of your footsteps. Be mindful of everything around you. Be grateful for all your senses. Be grateful you can think or taste and for all your senses while you play on this beautiful golf course. If you consciously set up this intention, before even getting to the golf course, before you start playing the game, then maybe you can be more conscious, and enjoy everything with more purity. Being mindful and conscious of your senses and your thoughts brings you back to the present. Be mindful all the way through the eighteen holes or nine holes, instead of wasting time thinking or worrying about what lies in the future or the past.

You are no longer just chasing a ball; playing golf is helping you connect internally with yourself and externally with everything around you. If you keep trying to do this, you will be living mindfully at the course. You may eventually find yourself living more thoughtfully or mindfully every day. You will then meet the true master of yourself and choose to create each moment differently. Mindfulness is a method and a tool to discover your inner master. Or: Mindfulness is a master that will help you to meet and discover your true self.

Reflection

How do you separate golf and home? Or do you have the same mindful awareness on the course and at home? Can you bring your mindfulness on the course to your home and work?

Jesse

MINDFULNESS, to me, means a thoughtful awareness of the effects of my thoughts or actions on myself, others, and the space around me. It is also a thoughtful appreciation of where I am or what I have.

In the golf world, I believe most people would consider mindfulness on the golf course to be good golf etiquette. When you watch professional golf or you play with regular golfers, you become aware of a respectful behavior that allows everyone playing to enjoy their game without interference from each other, even though the players are sharing the same space. For example, other players are quiet and stand away from your line of vision when you are hitting your shot; players walk around each other's ball on the green so as not to step on their line to the hole; and they yell "fore" if their ball is heading toward another player unaware of the incoming errant ball. To a regular golfer this is a common-sense part of the game, but to a new golfer this is not yet in their awareness. The newbie golfer is so focused on their struggle to hit the ball in the correct direction, and so worried about holding up play, that they may play out of turn or walk ahead of another person playing a shot. Their ego is wrapped up in trying to avoid appearing incompetent or not wanting to be a bother, so they cannot be aware of anyone else's needs in their space. An accomplished player can fall into the same behavior if they are not playing up to their standard and they get frustrated. Their ego gets upset, and they may act out in anger, or get absorbed in self-pity, or when playing well, they may forget their playing partners, walk ahead, or talk about themselves when others are trying to focus. Getting wrapped up in the ups and downs of ego can lead to mindless behavior affecting the atmosphere and flow of the game for everyone around you.

But being mindless not only affects everyone and the space around you; it directly affects you, too. Golf is a wonderful game to practice mindfulness. Good golf requires a positive mindset and positive focus—which begin with yourself. One focus of being mindful is learning to be in the present and to be able to redirect your thoughts when they want to leave the "now" and return to the past or project into the future. This is an aspect of my game that I am constantly working on, thanks to Nadine sharing with me how she would work on this when she was competing. She was tired of the stress and noticed how exhausted every round of golf seemed to make her, from worrying about the things that may happen or hanging on to thoughts of past mistakes. She began a journey of paying attention to her thoughts and making a clear decision to take the reins, like training a child to take the correct path. When walking down the fairway or approaching the next shot, if a thought from her ego-self projected a fear of the bunker on the left, a hazard short of the green, or the pulled shot on that same hole yesterday, she would gently remind her ego-self that it was irrelevant to the task at hand, which was to focus on her swing routine and link it to the target. At first it was a constant effort to redirect all the time, but as her ego-self got used to the correction, it seemed to get quieter and Nadine found it easier to be present—literally for every moment over the ball. I'd caddy for her sometimes, and I could notice a different focus level the more she improved at this mindful skill. A hidden bonus was that I learned to become a more thoughtful caddy in my communication, and I was able to transfer this habit to my own game.

Have you noticed times when you are preparing to start a swing—and your thoughts change to visualizing hitting it in the hazard in front of the green? This is your mind projecting your fear of a possible future result that doesn't actually exist in the present moment. Do you remember a time when a memory from a previous hole of hitting the ground before the ball pops into your head as you are about to hit an approach shot to the green? This is your ego reminding you of a failure that happened in the past, and again this has no relevance to the present moment you are in. How about a time when you hit a ball and then the first thought or words out of your mouth are "You idiot. You're terrible at this game," or "I don't know why I bother"? These thoughts or words carry energy forward and have consequences to your demeanor and ability on your next shot, because you are reinforcing the idea that you are not good at this task. It also carries negative energy that affects the atmosphere for those you are playing with. Both mindfulness and mindlessness are like stones thrown in water; the ripples continue to affect the water far from the point of the stone's entrance. You can practice being mindful of your effect on yourself and others by being aware of these thoughts in your mind and choosing to change your response to them. You can reject those ideas as irrelevant to the moment and choose a different thought or response. Be kind to yourself, just like you would talk to a child that needs redirection.

This is practicing being mindful of what you are thinking and how it affects your experiences. I have learned that this is not easy and takes discipline, but it brings me back to the goal of being my own master on the course and in my life. To be a master means directing yourself positively and noticing when you fall victim to self-destructive thoughts or behaviors.

Do you remember in the 2010 *Karate Kid* where the young student learned the discipline of hanging up his jacket instead of dropping it on the floor? Through this training he learned this mindful habit had positive consequences for his mother, who no longer had to tidy up after him, and it created a mindfulness of looking after his belongings because they have value and purpose and should be treated with respect and gratitude. And, of course, he also learned some kung fu moves too! There are many ways to practice mindfulness, and you can practice it on and off the golf course.

At home my wife is always reminding my son and me to be mindful of putting things away when we are done using them, because it leaves a nicer, clean environment for others in the house. We are teaching our son to be mindful of the words he uses to describe his feelings about others, or his experiences, because they carry an energy beyond that sentence and affect his own feelings and those around him. On the golf course, I am working on the mindfulness of staying present over every shot because it offers complete focus and clear intention for my energy. I also love to be mindful to enjoy my surroundings when I am out there. I am mindful to notice the beautiful cut of the fairway, the reach of the trees to the sky, and the gentle touch of the wind on my face. It reminds me to be thankful for the opportunity to be out there and to be thankful for the team that put in the effort to keep the golf course in the condition it is for us to enjoy. I think this is the reason I love to take the opportunity to join the grounds crew to cut the grass some days, as it gives me the chance to create the beauty I see every day.

It is a pleasure to play with a person who is mindful of themselves, their effect on others, and the space around them, and far more enjoyable to play golf that way yourself. At first it requires self-discipline to be aware of your own thoughts and behaviors, but as you do pay attention you will notice that it spawns an energy of gratitude and relaxation. It is easier to notice mindfulness, or the absence of it, in someone else when playing golf, but it takes awareness and practice to notice its absence within yourself and choose to retrain your reactions and your inner dialogue when you are playing.

We are all sometimes unaware of our habits. When we become aware of a habit that does not benefit our game or those around us, then we can choose to make a change, and that is mindfulness. It might seem overwhelming to do this all the time at first, so choose a small way to begin your evolution to mindfulness. It could be a simple start like deciding to remember to be aware of the warm feel of the sun on your skin or the cool touch of the wind when you are outside. You will notice that when you start this small practice it will expand to other things, because it rewards you with a warm, peaceful feeling that you will want to expand on. Then as you relax with this mindful moment, you might start to notice your thoughts and become mindful of wanting to change or redirect the less positive ones, one at a time. Another small way to develop mindful behavior and thinking is by fixing a pitch mark on the green, created by a ball landing on the soft surface. When you repair the dent in the green, be aware that you are helping the roots of the grass heal; be aware of the beauty of the smooth putting surface that the grounds crew try to create for you; and be mindful of providing a nice surface for the people behind you to putt on. This is a rewarding mindful behavior because you become part of creating and maintaining the wonderful environment where you enjoy playing the game.

Mindfulness in golf is not necessarily being perfectly positive all the time, but instead noticing when we are thinking or doing something that does not perpetuate positivity—and choosing to change that habit. We are all aware of the thoughtless or mindless behavior of young children, and we're patient to teach them a more thoughtful or mindful way to respond, so why don't we continue this practice as adults? It takes practice, but it's a valuable awareness tool that will grow your enjoyment of the game and help you reach your golfing goals, with happier memories and happier friends sharing your space. When we get better at being mindful of ourselves, it becomes easier to be mindful and more compassionate toward others.

As I write this chapter, I am mindful of how happy I am to share this collaboration with Geshe-la with you and others like you, who want to create a more positive world for yourselves and others, and to start that journey together with our love of the great game of golf.

Reflection

I love playing golf by myself sometimes. I love the quiet opportunity it gives me to work on self-awareness and enjoy the beauty in my surroundings. If you have this opportunity to play by yourself, challenge yourself to be mindful of your thoughts and self-talk in a round of golf. Once you notice the destructive thought processes happening, you can correct your habits with more productive conversations with yourself. Take time to notice how the thoughts of the past or possible future (good or bad) affect your body and emotions. Do you feel calm and focused, or apprehensive, unsure, or full of adrenaline? Realize that neither the past nor the future needs to affect the present, and you can gently bring yourself back to the process at hand. Being mindful takes practice in self-awareness and empowers you with more productive thoughts and actions rather than operating on mindless reactions. Be your own master!

10. Visualization

I am clear about where I want to be.

When I am really clear and know my vision, I will achieve it, sooner or later

If you are not really clear in your head and heart, then the results will be unclear as well

When you can clearly visualize your own life, you can also clearly visualize a golf ball

The power of clarity will naturally take us where we want to go.

—Geshe-la

Geshe-la

VISUALIZATION PRACTICE is a part of the spiritual training and practice of my Yung Drung Bon tradition of Tibet. We believe this is a method of transformation to a higher level of consciousness. I studied numerous profound teachings on this philosophy for many years. But my first occurrence of visualization was visualizing my master Jawob Rinpoche.

One time when I was a teenager my master and other monks came to my uncle's house for a couple of days in order to perform rituals and blessings. I used to watch my master's face, especially when he sat quietly and closed his eyes. I don't know if he was meditating or thinking, but I loved watching his face. When I closed my eyes, I could see his face very clearly, the arch of his eyebrows, his wrinkles, and the set of his mouth. Beyond the physical form I could see his gentleness, compassion, and loving kindness. Even today, every time I do guru yoga practice, I see his face and feel his presence and inner qualities. I connect right away.

Visualization is very powerful. When I was a teenager it transformed the usual teenage emotions and challenges into a feeling of blessing and gratitude. I felt that every good thing that happened to me was because of my teacher's blessing. This connection to him changed my life, and my practice is strong today because of him.

Later when I came to Canada, I became very ill. The pain in my stomach was so strong that I had to go to the emergency room. Aside from the pain, it was quite frightening because I struggled to understand the English being spoken around me. I was told my appendix needed to be removed, but I really had no clue what was involved. But the doctor was clear that I needed surgery, so I signed a piece of paper I didn't understand and gave him permission to proceed. I had never had a surgery before.

I had no power; only the doctor had the wisdom and the knowledge of what to do. I could only trust the universe; if it was my karma to live, I would. If not, something else would happen. I trusted completely and let go.

I had been given a painkiller and to calm myself I visualized my master's face and focused on that as I was pushed on a gurney from room to room. When I went into surgery I smiled at the doctors and heard them comment, "He's smiling!" It wasn't what they expected. I remained focused on my master's face, and the surgery seemed to pass quickly. All was well afterward.

This powerful tool of visualization is useful when one finds oneself in a negative emotional state like anger or loneliness. Visualizing positive images, such as spiritual beings or even a puppy dog, can change one's mind from something negative to positive. Whatever brings you joy and blessings—feel that, become that. Visualize that your goals are accomplished and plant that intention in the universe without attachment. When it's ready to happen, it will happen. Whatever you're going through, practice visualization. For me, whenever I visualize my master's face, I have a spontaneous connection, without effort, and it brings me peace. I have done this my whole life, and I am grateful.

Part of my traditional practice is transformation through visualization. This is very important to do occasionally, even daily if you can.

You can transform your consciousness and energy to be more positive by visualizing positive things. For example, if you imagine a place where you wish to be, it can be as though you are right there. You can also imagine that you have all the qualities of the person you wish to be. When you visualize being that person, something of your mind, or your consciousness, becomes that. Right then. At that moment any negative thoughts, feelings, or energy transforms into positive energy and positive thinking.

Visualization can be applied to anything, including golf. Before you get to the golf course, it is important to mentally visualize each hole. See where you want to be and where you want to hit. You can imagine how many pars or birdies or bogeys you will get. Mentally go to each hole as best you can remember them; when you do this, it's as though you planted, or seeded, your vision. You plant the seed and then, when you get there, you already have a plan mapped out. When you plant the seed energetically and mentally, there is a subtle energy you can put there. It is very powerful. The more times you can play in your imagination, the more familiar you become, and the next time you play that course it is easier to play. You can also visualize each aspect of the game, such as how you want to swing, and which club you'll use. You can visualize that you are a pro you really admire and visualize their swing and the way they hit. Then transform yourself into being that player. This is a way to get to where you want to be and play the game you want to play.

Reflection

Do you visualize the course before you play it? If so, what does that look like?

How about your life—do you visualize where it is heading?

Jesse

VISUALIZATION IS such a powerful tool. It's a tool that all great athletes use, as do people who are very successful in other aspects of life. We all can daydream, and we have all had a moment where we see ourselves achieving something great. That is the beginning of visualization. When a painter starts to paint, they have already created the image in their head, and they transcribe it with their paintbrush. When we play golf, we can create the shot in our minds and transcribe it with our chosen club. Unfortunately, we seem more prone to see negative images in our head, and focus on the things we are afraid of or the areas we want to avoid.

In the chapter "Mindfulness," we discussed the importance and awareness of giving your mind something positive to focus on, so that the negative can't fill that space in your head. Visualization is a great way to do this. Over the years, I have gotten better at developing this skill, but I used to be more like the players that allowed the punishing obstacles on the course to drive their direction and energy. My wife can attest that I would create my own negative story with each shot. If I hit a shot off my target line and ended up in the rough, I would literally say, "What a nightmare!" before I even got to see where the ball ended up. In my head, I had already created a picture of my ball having a bad lie resulting from that last poor shot, leading to a bogey. "Nightmare" was a common word in my rounds of golf, and the energy and images it created in my head and in my body were stressful and destructive. My wife kept telling me that I was creating my own reality, and she was right.

I remember the day this habit started to change for me. It was a tournament round at MetroWest Golf Club in Orlando, Florida, and I was on the tenth hole and 4 over par. I had hit my second shot, on a par 5, into the greenside bunker. As per usual, I was already projecting how difficult it was going to be to get the birdie I so desperately wanted on that hole. When I reached my ball, I realized that it was plugged in the sand, close to the lip of the bunker. As I looked at the predicament of this next shot, something curious happened. I got a clear picture in my head of me popping the ball up onto the green successfully, using a three-iron! I pulled my three-iron out of my bag and as I did a few practice swings beside the bunker, I could feel how I needed to swing the club with a very open clubface down through the sand to pop the ball out. I could feel it and see it and felt very confident about my prospects of pulling this shot off. I did it! My ball popped softly up out of the bunker and finished a foot from the hole. What an amazing feeling that was, and I made my birdie despite the "bad" lie of my ball in the bunker. I continued to play the back nine with much greater success. More importantly I was excited at my awareness of this connection to my visual creativity and the feel in my hands and body. It was as if my whole system was communicating the plan so clearly.

From that day on, I realized that I had to make a change to my negative projections on the golf course. I practiced having the patience to check out the shot conditions when I arrived at the ball and getting a clear sense of the optimal play. By not projecting my frustrations on missed shots onto this one, I allowed myself time to evaluate the ball's situation with a clear mind and see it as a blank canvas ready for me to paint the next shot. I could see the lay of the grass, slope of the land, or trajectory needed to get the ball to its optimal next landing spot. The more I got into the details, the more my mind's eye could see the potential and the shot image I could create. This sent messages instantly to my hands and body of what it would need to feel like. It is the most amazing experience when you are able to feel this happen—it has a spiritual feel, and it is what many athletes refer to as being in the zone.

Sometimes it happens almost by mistake, just like it did for me at the MetroWest Golf Club. You might recognize that you can feel the shot happen before it does—like when you holed a chip shot from off the green and you said to your friends that you felt like you knew that was going to happen. It was like a visual premonition.

This really is a skill that everyone can home in on and practice all of the time. Think of yourself as a computer that needs to be programmed before it can do the task you need it to perform. The next time you play, no matter what your skill level might be, take a bit of time to really pay attention to the conditions of the lie of your ball: the lay of the grass, the slant of the ground, the space you have for the trajectory of the shot, and even the wind. Allow the conditions to help you interpret the shot you need to create and see it happen in your mind's eye. The more detailed you can make the image, the better—see the ball fly or roll out, and see the speed, the landing, and where it finishes. You will notice that the image sends a message to your body, and your practice swings will be able to mimic the shot to come. You'll be able to execute the shot with relaxed confidence.

The amazing thing with this practice is that even when the execution may not be perfect, the results are still better than without using this type of mental preparation. Enjoy your creativity, and the more often you do it, the faster your mind and body will connect to the process. It is a beautiful thing!

Visualization of the shot is an important part of my pre-shot routine from the tee box to the hole. I encourage you to adopt this process too. Stand behind your ball to pick your target line, see the ball flight in your mind's eye, and then connect that picture to your practice swing behind the ball. Step into the ball, still feeling the connection to that target-line picture, and allow your swing to perform the task you have programmed in your brain. I find this especially helpful with chipping and putting as you can clearly see the lay of the land and can picture the bounce and roll of the ball all the way to the hole. The more detailed and accurate the information you can see in your mind, the better the performance becomes. When I stand behind a putt, I visualize and sense the ball rolling on the green at a particular speed and on a certain path to allow the slope of the green to feed my ball into the hole. It is important to finish your picture with the ball falling into the cup. Do not stop short of the hole or past it, but see it fall into the bottom of the cup.

There are some days when your visualization and feel will be more in tune than others, but it is good to practice this as a functional part of the shot process each time you hit a golf shot. There are some days when I feel off balance in my swing and tempo, but I feel like I can "will" the ball around the course with my inner creative energy. We all have the ability to daydream, and no, it is not a waste of time. It is a skill that should be practiced and honed as an integral part of your game. I even encourage my son to daydream as often as he can, instead of getting lost in technology. I encourage you to even use it on the driving range: Imagine a seven-iron shot starting right of the flag and drawing in to drop down beside it, or imagine your driver starting down the left side with a gentle fade into the flag on the right. Have fun seeing these shots and then focusing on making them happen. Children play like this all the time. Learn to play and create while you play golf. For me, it is the best part of the game.

Reflection

Do you recall a time when you knew you were going to hole a chip or putt? Or do you recall a time when you knew you were going to chunk a shot into the hazard? This is self-determining visualization, and I know you would prefer to program the positive result rather than the negative.

The next time you play, pay attention to your thoughts as you walk up to your ball. See if you can take charge of this natural ability and program your mind and body for success. You begin with your putting. Take the time to read the line of your putt and imagine the ball rolling at a particular speed all the way into the hole. If you have a difficult time seeing a clear picture, just move your eyes along the green surface at the speed you think the ball should roll into the hole. Always complete the picture. This skill will improve your green-reading skills and help with your touch on the greens, too.

11. Befriending the Elements

We drink your water,
we breathe your air,
we walk on your earth,
we receive your fire as heat,
we are gracing your space,
you are all our true friends, because you create
me and everyone else,
you nurture us to grow strong through life,
you embrace us all, equally,
without your kindness and care, we won't survive,
therefore, we are forever grateful.

—Geshe-la

Geshe-la

IN 2009, I WAS INVITED to an International Indigenous Leadership Gathering in Lillooet, British Columbia. This gathering included spiritual leaders from around the world, including from Greenland, the South Pacific, Europe, Asia, and North and South America.

The idea for this gathering came to Chief Darrell Bob in a vision after a period of fasting and purification. He envisioned Indigenous leaders from around the world meeting and sharing cultural perspectives. I was grateful to be invited to this event, which celebrated sacred children, sacred generations, sacred knowledge, and sacred lands.

Every elder I heard spoke about the importance of the five elements and how to take care of and respect the spirits of the land and elements. All speeches came down to that.

What are the five elements? Different traditions might define them in different ways. According to the ancient Bon tradition, which is my lineage, they are these: space, wind or air, fire or heat, water, and earth. They are the foundation not just of the outside world but of our life, health, prosperity, mental confidence, and reputation. Without this foundation we cannot live; there would be no life. Therefore, it is very important to connect to them spiritually, mentally, and even scientifically.

If you are looking for the best supporter, helper, or

friend, then the most important friends that you can connect with are the five elements. Regrettably, through the destruction of the land and because of the impact of technology, we may become blocked from understanding that we are a part of the elements, and they are a part of us.

Your bone is the space element, your breath is the wind or air element, your heat is the fire element, your blood is the water element, and your flesh is the earth element. Our organs are connected to the elements too: The heart is the space element, our lungs are the wind or air, the liver is fire, kidneys are water, and the spleen is the earth element. Our senses are also connected to the five elements: the eye with space, nose with wind, tongue with fire, ears with water, and our body's feeling with earth.

Our internal balance of elements—our life force, health, prosperity, reputation, and mental confidence—depends on the external five elements, and they are interdependent. It is therefore so important to connect to the outside elements, to be friends with them and to be mindful of them. Then life can be beautiful, and your game of golf can be powerful.

When I look at players at the golf course, they are often fighting or resisting the elements. They fight with the water—the rain in their face, the water traps—because they fear it and therefore don't like it. Think of relationships between people, or even animals. If you don't like somebody, then they don't like you either. If you like somebody and you are nice to them, then they will eventually or immediately feel the same way toward you. That's the nature of life. Some people don't like the bunker, which is the earth element. Some people don't like the wind for the way it affects the ball, so they resist it and fight against it.

Instead of fighting the elements like enemies, you can welcome them as friendly parts of your game and your life. When you are playing golf, if you respect that each of these elements exists, then they will play with you and your ball, but they won't fight with you. You can trust them instead. When there is a water hazard in front of the green and you say to yourself, "I don't like this water," then you are afraid that your ball will not make it over the water, and your energy is focused on fighting it. Your mind is stuck on your fear, and you forget the green, the hole, the target. In a subtle way you are stuck with the water in fear and fighting. Instead, see the water as unified with the hole, and see how it hydrates the green, and see that they are not separate and there is no difference. Now the water is smiling and guiding you and will help you see the green, your target.

When you form this mindset first, as a foundation, then your energy is focused productively on your target instead of getting stuck fighting a fear. It is important that you don't fight anything, but befriend everything around you, including the scorecard, the other golfers, and the five elements. They are all beautiful. They all support you. Maybe your playing partners are your competitors in the game, but if your mindset is to see everything and everyone as helping you be the best you can be, then you are not wasting energy fighting the competition and are totally focused on being the best you can be. A friend is more powerful and beneficial than an enemy. An enemy can destroy you, and friends can support you and develop you, helping you improve yourself, and everything around you. Truly we are made of the elements.

In order to balance the five elements, prepare before you go to the course so that you will have a clear state of mind. First, fully recognize how your energy is at the present moment. Is your energy high or low? Are you feeling calm or agitated? Second, relax your shoulders and breathe slowly and deeply, and release. Do this three times. Meditate for a few moments. Third, recognize the stillness and clarity of your mind; feel the balance in your body. Next, feel the clarity and stillness around you. Be fully present and aware of the balance between you and the space around you. Be mindful of all the five elements around you, acknowledge them, and be their friend. Feel the stillness, clarity, focus, and confidence within and surrounding you.

If you hold this balanced space within, it cannot be destroyed. As well as helping your golf game, this balance can be brought with you to work or used in your relationships. The energy of balance can make a big difference to your life.

Reflection

When you come across a water hazard, a bunker, or another challenge on the course, be mindful of your reaction. Many people experience fear or resistance and end up fighting with these barriers instead of making them their friend. Can you see this as an opportunity to practice with difficult challenges?

We all face many obstacles in our life. Obstacles challenge us and can make us learn new ways of doing things. Life is not boring, because of the many challenges we face. Do you prefer challenges in your life or no challenges at all?

Jesse

PEOPLE WHO LOVE to play golf love the outdoors. They love to be outside, in touch with the elements of our world. Nonetheless, sometimes we find ourselves fighting against them or protecting ourselves from them.

I remember playing in the Canadian PGA Tour Qualifying event in Kamloops, Canada, back when I played competitive tour golf, on a day when the playing conditions of the morning rounds were far more favorable than the afternoon—and I happened to get an afternoon draw. The morning was sunny and dry with a breeze, while the afternoon competitors were presented with wind and a rainstorm. The leading scores of the morning round were quite low, with two course records set of 62, but my mindset was positive; I knew that I had lots of experience playing in tough weather conditions. With patience and appropriate equipment, I believed I could manage a good round despite the conditions.

There was no room on the driving range when I started to warm up, so I decided to use the driving range practice bunker to hit some irons; I had decided that I would use an iron off the first tee to place my drive in the best position possible. However, as I approached the first tee, the wind started to pick up, and as I watched the group ahead of me hit their shots, I changed my mind on what club to use—four times. I finally set my mind on hitting a driver straight into the howling wind.

The golf course was looking very different from the one I had played in my practice round the day before. I was shaken and uncomfortable and started the day with a 7 on the first hole. I knew I needed patience, and as the weather got worse with heavy rain adding to heavy winds, I added equipment to arm myself against what felt like the unfair onslaught from the heavens.

By the seventh hole I was 4 over par and tired of holding a blustering umbrella and trying to keep myself and my equipment dry against the unrelenting rain. It was at that moment that I resigned myself to acceptance. I decided to put away the umbrella, stop trying to keep everything dry, and just get wet. My body relaxed and I just focused on each shot at hand. Like a child, I felt the wind blow against my body and felt the rain across my face, and I adjusted my game to what I felt, without the extra energy to fight against it. I finished that round with a 76—not good enough to be competitive in the event, but under the circumstances I felt proud of that score and with what I had learned. Yes, it was unfortunate that I drew the afternoon torrential tee time, but it was a learning experience that has helped form my vision of the world.

From that day on, I am mindful of not complaining about the weather conditions but rather accepting them and listening to the information they give, so that I can play the best shot for that moment. It was the beginning of me developing my relationship with the elements and seeing them as my friends rather than my adversaries.

I grew up knowing four main elements: water, air, earth, and fire.

Water: See water as a friend, even in the form of rain. When it falls on you, it tells you that it is heavy and cold (or warm, or light) and lets you know that it is falling equally upon your ball; you will need more club to get it to your target. The course will play longer and slower, so just embrace your friend and play it as it feels, instead of begrudging it all day.

Water has a bad reputation on the golf course as golfers associate it with hazards. Start rethinking that relationship and see it as your friend. Water is hydrating for you and for the golf course, keeping it green and lush; quite often, hazards on the course are used as a water source for irrigation or as a drainage system to keep the fairways dry. They are a friend to the golf course and to the quality of the lie of your ball on the ground. Also, on a breezy day, the ripples on the water around the green will show you wind direction and speed, giving you important information to choose your shot. Hazards on the golf course are also used to frame the hole, adding beauty and definition to the landing areas, and giving accurate distance markers to reach your target. The landing areas stand out higher and bolder because of them, giving you a clearer target to aim at.

Water can also be calming to look at and soothing when you drink it. I often drink water if I am nervous or feeling anger and frustration. As I enjoy it, smooth coolness quells the fire inside and resets my energy for more fluid thoughts. The element of water is clearly a reliable friend.

Air: There is nothing better than breathing in some beautiful fresh air after a long day in the office; often, we can't wait to get to the golf course to enjoy it. But with air comes wind.

Golfers stay in tune with the wind all the time. We will toss a piece of grass into the air to see which way the wind is blowing and how hard. We watch the wind blow the trees and grass to get a measure on how far it might blow the ball off line and which club we should use to reach the target. However, we tend to be fickle friends with the wind and only like it when it is gentle or when we think it helps us, like when we can hit a long drive downwind, or when the wind helps blow the ball away from the hazard.

I encourage you to appreciate the wind for what it is in any condition. It's always giving you information to help you; even on the windiest days, don't fight it—just accept it as an element of your next shot. You can decide to hit a longer club or take the opportunity to learn how to hit a low shot under the wind and below the tree line. Most professionals love to practice into a head wind, as it accentuates the spin on the ball and can show errors in clubface and path. Wind encourages you to learn better ball-flight control and can be used to create softer shots into the green by shaping shots into the wind. Stop using your energy to fight against the wind on the course, and instead, embrace it as your friend and learn to work with it. You will find that the element of air, whether in the form of wind or as a deep, cool inhale of breath that energizes and relaxes you, is a friend just waiting to be acknowledged and appreciated.

Earth: Taking a walk can be grounding when you are

having a stressful day. The feel of the ground under your feet and the rhythm of your steps can be relaxing and calming.

The earth element on the golf course is a great friend when playing golf. When you look down the hole, the lay of the land shows you the direction. The slope of the fairway and green shows you the bounce and roll of the ball. The firm or soft feel of the ground under your feet tells you the degree of bounce or speed of the ball when it hits the ground. The slope you feel under your feet on uphill or downhill lies tells you if your shot will shape to the left or right or take off high or low. When you walk on the green you can feel the slope with your body to help read the greens. The earth is a friendly element on the course, full of helpful information, and has a grounding quality to help you find balance and relaxation. The earth element is a powerful friend that can calm you with the beauty of its shape on the ground and on the horizon. It holds you steadfastly as you take each step and provides you with useful information about what lies ahead.

Fire: Fire is not as obvious an element on the golf course as the others, but it is one we can feel. The sun is a source of the fire element on the course and in general it is very popular. We love the sun. It is warm and the heat feels good to our bodies and helps the ball go further, because warm air is less dense than cold air. It also makes the grass and trees grow, keeping the course vibrant and healthy for us to enjoy.

However, we have another source of fire in golf: The passion in our hearts for the game. When you watch players at the golf course, you can see the fire of passion burning bright. Sometimes this passion-fire can be a source of self-destruction when a player becomes too attached to their score instead, but generally the fire in our bellies is our friend that brightens our day and gives us focus and a passion to learn.

The element of fire is our friend that helps our health, brightens our mood, and allows growth of life on this planet.

Reflection

Do you see the elements when you play golf? What emotions do they evoke in you? For example: Do you look at the water as a friend or foe?

Try looking at the elements on the course as friends to be accepted and embraced, even when their temperament might be tougher on some days than others. The slope of the green (earth) leads to the hole. The wind in the trees (air) shows you which way to aim. The water hazards (water) define the perfectly cut fairway like a runway. The sun (fire) warms your body and helps you relax.

12. Compassion for Others

Sometimes, let go of your own pain
Try to focus on others' enjoyment and success
Sometimes, let go of yourself
To pay attention to another person's feeling
Sometimes, let go of your score

Focus on someone's journey of life
Sometimes, let go of falling apart
Focus on kindness for yourself and to others
Suffering can be the medicine of spiritual
awakening

—GESHE-LA

Geshe-la

I AM GRATEFUL TO have had many wonderful role models whose positive impact on my life has changed who I am today.

In particular, my spiritual mother Amala Norma Forrest was pivotal for my life in Canada. Amala was born in England during World War II. When she was four years old, she came to Canada; her mother was English and her father was a Canadian soldier. She was around sixty-five years old when I first met her, and she had already raised three children. This was in Terrace, British Columbia, in 1999.

The moment I first met her I felt embraced by her warm-hearted presence. I recognized her immediately as a loving and compassionate being. She was the first person I had met in the West in whom I saw this energy. I didn't really understand it completely, but I felt a true motherly love from her. When I first came to the West, I had felt at a distance from people. It's hard to understand, but sometimes I would be hugged but feel a little uncomfortable. Her hugs, however, felt straight from the heart: loving and kind. I felt a deep connection with her.

She invited me to her meditation group in Kitimat, and soon I began teaching Buddhism and meditation on a weekly basis. Every week she brought me tea and cookies. She took care of me and was protective of me.

Later I asked her if she would adopt me as a spiritual

son. I had lost my own mother when I was five. She was very surprised and asked if this was possible. I said yes! So we had a ceremony establishing our relationship.

I spent seventeen years with her until her death. She supported me financially and taught me how to understand Western culture. I had felt like a newborn in Canada; so much was unfamiliar, including the language. There are really no words to describe the way she nurtured and loved me.

I saw her extend her loving kindness to all kinds of people who came to my teachings. It was like she held the whole group in a warm, expansive hug. New people who weren't sure how to act were greeted wholeheartedly and taught how to be comfortable in the group. There was nothing of the self in this, just pure kindness and openness. Particularly when someone was unhappy or unfriendly she would go and sit with them. Whatever was blocking them inside, she would help open up. She held no expectations, but her open heart and mind were powerful in helping people.

I learned so much from seeing her powerful compassion embrace everyone. I saw how powerful it is to not focus on oneself but to focus on others and what we can do for them and not just for ourselves.

When we play golf or any sport, or really do anything, we often focus on our own self—on our own feelings, our own ideas, or our own goals and wishes—instead of the other person's wishes, goals, or feelings. It would be really nice if we could practice compassion for others some days, if not all the time.

For me this means that I want whoever I golf with to have a wonderful game. I want them to have a good score, and I focus on supporting them in some way. I enjoy focusing on playing as well as I can when I complete a shot, but my experience on the golf course is so much bigger than that. When I add up all the time I'm focused on my own shot execution, it's a very small portion of the time that I'm on the course. In between shots, I find it productive and joyful to spend that time focused on the other players in my group. I get to enjoy their good shots with them or share in their despair when they mishit a shot.

My focus is with them instead of on my own past shots. It's not positive to stay focused on your own good or bad shots; that's how your ego keeps you self-involved. Instead, focus on the opportunity to connect with others and show compassion for them and yourself. Focusing on someone else's enjoyment or success is more peaceful and joyful than focusing on ourselves. The more we focus on ourselves, the unhappier we become; the more we focus on others' happiness, the happier we are. Then, our intention is not for ourselves to be happier, but that's nonetheless what happens when our focus and behavior is for the betterment of others.

You can play golf with people and not make a connection with them at all. On the other hand, when you pay attention to the energy and feelings of those in your group, the conversation flows easier, and everyone becomes more relaxed and open. If you notice that another person seems stuck in a negative state, try to connect with that player and their feelings, thinking "I know your feelings." Allow them time for their mind to shift. Then maybe you can change the subject or find something else to do. You will find the perfect time, the perfect moment, the perfect way to say what you want to say, when you consider the other person's feelings.

At the end of the day, what matters is to be joyful and peaceful, not how well you play the game of golf. What matters in life is how it feels for others to be around you and your positive connection with other people. When you have a quiet moment on your own, it is special when you can remember a meaningful conversation or a moment of laughter and joy that brings a smile to your heart. This experience is more beautiful than focusing on your score or being angry or disappointed at a few bad shots. Instead, take the opportunity when you play with others to learn about them and about yourself and how to connect with compassion for others. I try to live my life with a focus of compassion for others and I find that golf offers such a wonderful environment to do that. Golf offers a great opportunity to practice compassion for others' successes and difficulties, as well as a beautiful space to share peace and kindness.

Reflection

If you see someone playing very well, how do you feel? What do you do? If you see someone playing poorly, how do you feel? What do you do?

Jesse

FOR A GOOD part of my life, I'm not sure I knew what it meant to really have compassion for others. I was more focused on competing, trying to be better than the person next to me, and feeling as if others had advantages over me. This is treating life like a survival game—a scarcity mentality where the strongest survive. Unfortunately, that attitude is mirrored by our society, where so many people are hooked on watching the misfortune of others because it makes them feel better about their own lives. This is a self-focused attitude and, as I have since realized, the opposite of compassion.

Each of us, at some point, has been taken advantage of or has felt invisible to the world, and those experiences can shut off one's compassion and the ability to connect with and see others clearly. It's as if we fear that if we spend energy or time focused on someone else, we will lose out on something for ourselves. I have learned that closing yourself off and holding on to your resources creates a lot of stress in the body. To counter those feelings and restore compassion, one of my favorite things to do is "pay it forward." When I'm in line at the coffee shop, going through the drive-through, I like to buy the person behind me their coffee. It is my way of having compassion for the person I don't know and, hopefully, bringing a smile and a feeling of being noticed to their day. I leave there with the hope that they will pay the feeling forward to someone else.

I had the great opportunity to play some golf with a major league baseball player, Ken Harrelson, when I was younger, and he shared some wisdom about the freedom compassion brings. He told me to take care of the ball when I played golf, to treat it with kindness. He told me never to hit a golf shot with stress in my hands. Instead, hit the ball with compassion and caring about where it needs to go.

When I focus on taking care of my ball, my mind slows, the shot becomes clearer, and my body softens to mindfully get the ball to where it belongs. The stress leaves my hands, and the need to slash at the ball with intensity dissipates. The angst and desperation go away, and the energy flows through me more effectively.

One way I remind myself to pay attention to this thought process is by marking my golf ball with "JJJ." These letters remind me of my brothers and me—Jacob, Jesse, and Jag—and now also my son, Javan Jag. It always reminds me of security in family and the compassion and love we feel. I encourage you to try this next time you play a round of golf. Maybe you could mark your ball with a symbol that connects with you.

Having compassion for my golf ball reminds me of an exercise I had to do at school where I had to look after an egg without breaking it. For a period of time, I had to be mindful of how I performed daily activities, and it made me slow down and be gentle by taking care of something outside of myself.

Treating the golf ball with compassion can be extended to also focusing on those around us when we play golf. I found that once I practiced treating my ball with compassion, my inner energy changed and my outlook toward others around me softened.

Start when you arrive at the golf course. Slow yourself down in the parking lot and as you walk into the pro shop, look at the people around you. Have compassion for how their day is going and be thoughtful about bringing something as simple as a smile to their day. When I play with others now, I try to treat them and their games like I do my own golf ball. I am open to sharing caring energy with them and wishing them well for their shots and their walk around the course. I hope they enjoy the birds and surroundings as much as I do, and I hope my warm energy helps them to relax and enjoy being there with me in that round. I always feel that I perform better and have a better perspective on the game when I adopt this mindset. I hope that the people at the course are happy and relaxed with those they are playing with, as in the end, your score does not matter as much as connecting with people and letting good energy flow.

If you ever feel tense or unsure at a golf course, take the time to breathe and see the people around you and those you are lucky to interact with. When you do this, notice how your insides relax, your breathing slows, and you become less obsessed by your own concerns. You may feel free and relaxed, ready to enjoy your round and your day. Good energy is abundant and flows freely when we open our minds to compassion. Have compassion for others. Have compassion for your golf ball. Have compassion for yourself. This will lead to better scores and a happier heart.

Reflection

How do you feel when you arrive at the golf course or on the first tee? How do you feel at the end of your round? Do you feel like you connected with your playing partner at all? In your next round of golf, try to extend compassion to your playing partners. Celebrate their good shots, have empathy for their poor shots, and feel how your own internal energy relaxes and flows. Energy is supposed to flow and when we try to bottle it up inside, it feels like stress. Positive, caring energy flows and returns in abundance, and your golf game will benefit greatly from that freeing feeling.

13. Self-Accomplishment

Being truly yourself is your first job
Trying to the best of your ability is your
accomplishment
Do not compare to another's level
Each person has his or her ability and that is
all that matters
Measure to your own standard

—Geshe-la

Geshe-la

I'VE HAD MANY wonderful people in my life, such as mothers, grandmothers, teachers, and uncles, who have taught me, loved me, and guided me. My youngest uncle, Tashi Jamay, the one who asked me to be a shepherd for him, was a very special man. He was a good person and a businessman with integrity. He always encouraged me to be successful, do good for others, and accomplish what I wanted. Even when I was ten years old, he would talk to me like an adult and discuss what's important in life. I really valued my time with him—though I didn't actually set specific goals at that time, other than education.

I do remember as a boy that I wanted to be really popular or famous when I grew up. When I came to Canada, I still had that desire to become famous. Then one day I was hiking with some friends on Mount Washington in British Columbia, and we discussed whether being famous was a good idea or not. My friend and student Robert pointed out, "Geshe-la, you're already kind of famous, but you don't want to be too famous; it's no good." As the discussion led to the many problems famous people can face, I really changed my perception. I thought, "Yeah, really famous people lose their freedom, and besides, what do I really want to accomplish?" I realized that I had already accomplished being a teacher, helping people, writing books, and playing golf to the best of my ability. Everything I do, I do to the best of my ability, and that is my accomplishment.

Each day I accomplish being who I am, doing my best and not measuring myself against others. When I was younger I didn't really measure my own ability; instead I looked at the accomplishments of others and judged myself against them. I thought I should be more like them. Now I'm content that I will perform to the best of my ability every hour, day, and week, every time. That is my accomplishment. I embrace that and no longer compare myself to others.

In golf, with my knowledge and ability, I can figure out distance and alignment. Then I hit the ball as well as I can, and then I watch and accept what happens. If my ability is less than someone's or more than someone else's, that is the karmic nature of life. I embrace and recognize that.

Accomplishment has no measure; it is infinite. We need to be aware of this because we often measure our success based on someone else's accomplishment, which can result in suffering or disappointment. Usually, it leads to disappointment and low self-worth.

It's always nice for people to have a role model or someone to look up to, someone who can give inspiration and encouragement as an example to follow. At the same time, it's important to pay attention and listen to yourself about your own capacity or ability in that particular activity. Some have the ability to become a billionaire, and some don't. If you have an attachment or expectation of being something that is not within your capacity to achieve, it can lead to disappointment and self-destructive attitudes and behavior. Instead, acknowledge the value of your own ability and focus on using it and developing it. Recognize your talent, set your own goals—not someone else's—and be grateful for what you are accomplishing on your own journey.

You'll notice that your level of ability may change on a daily basis. Some days you can do things better than you can on other days. If you have put in a good effort and find that you cannot do something as well as you thought, then accept that, and if you can, focus on something that you can achieve.

The same thing applies to golf. Be happy working with the ability you have instead of wanting to be something you are not, and then beating yourself up for it. Do the best you can, and then, even if the shot doesn't land the way you wanted it to, feel accomplished and satisfied with your commitment, effort, and level of achievement. If you keep doing that, whether in golf or any other sport, you will enjoy yourself and feel a sense of pride. Start with the intention to always try your best. You may get par that day or get a birdie that is your personal best. Celebrate these achievements instead of being disappointed because your playing partner got two birdies or hit the ball farther than you all day.

Competition can be good, because it propels us to perform better or try to be the best we can be, and competing can make us dig deeper to see what level of skills we have. You can check whether comparing yourself to someone else or competing with them in some way is positive or not by paying attention to your feelings. Is it creating a feeling that is joyful, peaceful, or meaningful?

Or does it create disappointment, anger, frustration, or unhappiness?

For any sport, and anything in your life, use this method of measuring your self-accomplishment, of measuring your ability against your own goal. Knowing your capacity or energy at the moment is important. Setting achievable short- and long-term goals and then adjusting them as you grow is important for positive growth and self-affirmation. Being too hard on yourself or beating yourself up is not a good method to live by. I believe that accomplishment is measured according to one's own ability.

Reflection

When you return home from golf, what are you thinking and feeling? Is your mind having slower patterns? Is your body tired? How is your energy? Are you still thinking about the game? Are you in a good mood because things went well? Or grumpy because they didn't? (I notice in myself that when my game is good, I feel accomplished and at peace.)

Jesse

WE ALL HAVE goals for our lives and for our passions, and they are important to have; they give direction and focus to the things we do. We need to be mindful of how we set our goals and how we prioritize them, or they can set us up for defeat. Looking back at my career in the game, if I could change anything it would be to set my goals differently.

When I started to really love the game of golf, my goal was to make it to the PGA Tour. A great goal to have, but a huge one that was a long way from the level I was at. And it meant that each tournament I played that I did not win, and each qualifying event I entered but didn't finish in the top four of two hundred people, felt like a failure. Those were defeats for my ego to bear, making my quest feel like an uphill battle.

Lots of players at the club level set score goals, like breaking 80 or breaking par. Many have goals like winning their club championship. There are endless goals in golf, such as your first birdie, first hole-in-one, longest drive, or best personal score in a tournament. These are all good goals, but they are specific moments in time that either make you feel great for the moment of achievement or feel defeated when you come close but don't quite finish the job.

I remember a competitive round I had at Windermere Golf and Country Club where I was 3 under par standing on the eighteenth hole and wanting to shoot a 69. Of course, I blew it, which is why it is now a part of this story. I hit it out of bounds on the right side and I could feel my heart just drop to my knees as the accomplishment I'd had in sight was gone in an instant. I forgot so quickly that I had played great golf for the first seventeen holes, because my ego was so focused on measuring myself by the goal of shooting a 69.

I think these types of goals are great if we focus on them like a "bucket list" of things that would be fun to accomplish—accomplishments that are fun bonuses to our journey. But I think we are better served by setting goals that are smaller, consistent, and more general to our daily performance process. Goals that are less ego driven and, rather, more principled and lifestyle driven.

When I play golf now, my goal is to be presently focused on each shot, to enjoy my walk and make the most of each challenge and opportunity I have on the course that day. My goal is to be the master at each shot I face; to take the lead as the creator in that moment, instead of the victim; and to accept the results as a learning opportunity, instead of making myself feel like a hero or a loser.

When I practice, my goal is to work on the swing changes I need to improve as a player. When I go to the course, I make a mental note of the aspects of my swing or short game that I need to improve upon. I give myself an image or feel that I want to accomplish, whether it be a shot pattern or a swing change or to improve my percentage of six-foot putts that I hole out. When I play, my goal is to be presently focused on each shot. Sometimes I even keep track on a scorecard or some paper as to how many shots I felt I was present and focused for, and sometimes I just play to enjoy the round. When I am done with my round, I can look back and feel good about enjoying the walk and about the focus I brought to each moment in my round.

I feel a sense of self-accomplishment from the focus that led to great shots and the presence that allowed me to learn from the shots I missed. I find this goal gives consistency to every day and a feeling of self-accomplishment to every round. This kind of goal builds my confidence and increases my comfort zone every day, as it grows my character and discipline. Whether I am playing or practicing, my goal is to be the manager and creator of my game. Every time I am successful at that I feel like a winner.

This is not a fleeting goal, but rather a goal to live by that never changes. I bring it to every golf course, every tournament, and every practice day.

A great athlete continues to be great before and after wins and losses; their wins are moments in time along their journey. You cannot control whether you win, or what the other athlete achieves, and you cannot always control your score. Why focus your goal on mastering something that's subject to so many variables? But you can master your focus, attitude, and presence on the course. These are things you can control to create effective change.

Consider this way you could approach your game daily, physically and mentally:

Each day have a focused physical goal of a specific aspect of your game. For instance, you may want to work on your putting skills; if so, for practice you could set thirty minutes aside to focus on six-foot putts. Or maybe you've noticed you'd like to hit more fairways off the tee, so you book a lesson to fix your slice or take some time to work on those swing mechanics. These are physically active goals. When you're done with the activity, you can feel accomplished that you set aside that time to work on those things. Feeling proud of your focused practice time builds confidence in your self-preparedness.

Also focus on your mental goals. Some examples: Take time to visualize each shot on the course, or pay attention to the details of your next shot: the wind, the slope of the ground, or the shape of the hole. Pay attention to your emotions on the golf course as well—choose to take a breath and be the master of the situation rather than the victim of circumstance.

These physical and mental goals create personal moments of self-accomplishment that build a consistent level of confidence and mastery over time. When you focus on achieving these types of goals, you'll be rewarded with consistent upliftment and pride in commitment. On the other hand, when you achieve some of your bucket-list achievements, like winning a tournament, reaching a particular handicap, or shooting a low score, the positive fulfillment is fleeting because it's just a moment; although it's exhilarating, it's not a lasting accomplishment.

You may even notice that this practice of consistent mastery spills over into other aspects of your life, and the feeling of self-accomplishment can be enjoyed every day.

REFLECTION

Have you finished a golf round and described it as a failure because you blew a good round with a double bogey on the seventeenth hole or something similar? Why disregard all the success you had on sixteen holes because one hole hurt your final-score goal?

I understand the concept of having a goal to shoot better scores, but tearing yourself down due to one mistake is not an effective way to achieve the result you want. This type of goal creates despair and disappointment before it is achieved, and the goal is fleeting. Consider paying attention to all the great things you did on the course and how much better you are getting at focus, relaxation, and creative play. This will build positive reinforcement and before you know it, you will be scoring better too. It will also change the negative-energy talk with your friends and family after the round. Choose to be a positive conductor of energy for yourself and others.

14. Anger

Anger is like a storm of inner emotion
Temporarily coming from within the emptiness of the mind
Arisen from causes, conditions of fear, hurts, attachment, expectations
It stays there and goes back to the same emptiness of mind
It can destroy the purity of inner qualities of a beautiful spirit, of flowers and health
But if we are protected and can build the walls of patience and the roof of awareness
and shine the light of kindness and compassion
We have the conscious choice to be in either the storm of inner darkness
or the sunshine of peacefulness and joyfulness
It's totally up to you: be the master, or not.

—Geshe-la

Geshe-la

When I was around thirteen years old, another village boy of the same age used to bully me. He made fun of my Bon spiritual tradition and of me. This really bothered me. One day, he pushed me down and continued to ridicule me. I was so angry. I got up and fought back. It was a big fight. Reflecting on it later, I was aware that I had lost myself; my anger changed who I was. I really wanted to hurt that boy.

Later as an adult, after I had come to Canada, a different situation made me very angry. It was during a phone call with one of my uncles. Throughout my life this uncle had given me a lot of advice and criticism that wasn't always helpful. I think he loves and cares for me, but he was very controlling and sometimes harsh. I had never said anything to him about it; I just obeyed him my whole life. Sometimes I felt more fear toward him than love and respect.

Even after I came to Canada, he would phone and tell me what to do. One day I just couldn't hold my feelings in anymore, and I started yelling at him over the phone. Today, I don't even remember why we were fighting, but I know I had no control over my anger. My whole body was shaking and afterward I was very hot. Later when I spoke with my uncle again he said that his body had been shaking too. There was huge physical distance between us, but we were connected through extreme mutual anger.

Thinking about this afterward really shook me up. I felt terrible that this huge, negative emotion of anger had temporarily destroyed my mind. I'd known that anger was considered one of the three poisons of Bon, along with ignorance and greed, but that had been more of a philosophical understanding. Only when it happened to me did I truly experience and understand the loss of control.

Even as an adult with training in spiritual practice, I could still lose myself. I felt so bad afterward; I needed to learn a different way. Since then I have changed myself and want to teach other people how to deal with anger in a positive way.

It's important to recognize and acknowledge how much is destroyed by anger. For instance, anger destroys the balance of our mental state. It blocks our awareness and changes our energy and emotions; we can change from being positive to being very negative. Physically it can result in high blood pressure or heart attacks.

We often think, "I have the right to be angry," in whatever situation or circumstances we find ourselves in. Sometimes we feel ashamed of our angry response, and it doesn't feel good, but we keep projecting our anger into the world anyway. When you're angry, it's like when you cut your finger. It's bleeding, and if you don't try to stop it, it will just keep bleeding, and then you are wounded. Instead, you should bandage it right away or see a doctor immediately to help resolve the problem. Similarly, when we're emotionally frustrated or angry, we must try to deal with it effectively in order to resolve the problem and not just let our anger bleed into the world. One of my commitments on the golf course is to not be angry, and if I do notice anger stirring within me, I transform it.

What causes anger? Where does it come from? There are three root causes of anger: a high or unreasonable expectation, attachment, and fear. When golfing, for instance, you may have an expectation of where you want the ball to go, how far you want to hit, or what your score will be. When you fail at this, then you may get angry—not because of the ball, the other golfers, the score, or the course, but because of your expectations.

Attachment happens when you become obsessed with what you want or when you have something you value. Think about a dog with a bone. When someone comes close or tries to take it away, it gets angry. On the golf course, you might be hitting the ball well, and all of a sudden you get a bad bounce, your ball goes into a hazard, and you make a double bogey. You were attached to the good score you thought you were going to have that day, and the bad bounce took that away from you. When you become attached to anything, you become easily angered by its loss.

Then there is fear. You might have a fear of losing something or someone or a fear of getting hurt. On the course, you might be scared that people may laugh at you or see you as incompetent. You might fear losing your new, better handicap that you finally reached. I have even seen people fear losing their ball or hitting into a hazard. This fear leads to anger because you feel vulnerable to attack or loss.

There are two types of anger: hot anger and cold anger. Hot anger is easy to see and includes yelling, a shaking body, a red face, and sometimes violent behavior. Some people have cold anger, which is not as obvious. Someone with cold anger could have a blue or gray face. They may appear frozen, like ice. They don't shout and yell but keep it inside. We often say, "I kept my cool"—that's cold anger. Both do damage.

The emotion builds as it goes through a process: first, impatience, then irritation, and then a tantrum. The process can take a minute, a second, or it could take hours or days. Eventually you become angry or enraged. Rage is a kind of madness, which means we have no ability to discern what is real anymore.

So how can we deal with anger? First, it's important to admit or acknowledge when we're angry. It's okay to be angry. Anger is natural, and everyone gets frustrated. You can acknowledge the anger, and say to yourself and others that you're angry. The second step is to avoid the object of your anger: the ball or the person or whatever you're angry about. Focus on something else, like breathing. Focus on something that brings you peace, like playing music, watching ducks in the pond, or anything else that makes you calm. Then, once you're in a more peaceful state, you can focus on compassion. Embrace yourself. Anger is an emotion from a hurt, so when you acknowledge your hurt with kindness to yourself, you can contemplate the situation and release the anger.

Reflection

How do you deal with anger? If you lose control of your emotions, what do you do when you're in that state? In golf, first pushing forward even harder usually makes things worse, so how do you rebalance yourself?

For me, when I feel my energy going down and that my expectations aren't being met, I still don't want to quit, so I focus on what is going well. For instance, I celebrate my one good shot and don't hold on to the bad. I may consciously change my mind and stop thinking about the score. I may think about how glad I am to be outside golfing and not stuck inside doing something unpleasant.

Jesse

WE HAVE ALL experienced anger in our lives, and it seems that everyone has a different boiling point. We teach our children that it's not acceptable to throw a tantrum when they don't get what they want, and we try as adults to not let anger control our behavior. Yet we do not always learn a constructive way to deal with this very real emotion.

On my journey as a golf professional, I have had plenty of experience of my own frustration or anger destroying my round. For instance: I've set up to a driver with the intention to send the ball straight down the middle and in position for a one-hundred-fifty-yard shot into the green. I felt a little off balance and uncomfortable in my setup but hit it anyway—and the ball went out of bounds on the right. The anger at myself boiled in my belly and head. I knew I should have pulled out of the shot before I hit it, but I swung the club anyway. I snatched another ball from my bag, teed it up in anger—and then tensed up on the swing for fear of repeating the same shot and continuing with anger throughout the hole and maybe the entire round. Sometimes this would affect my whole day. I have had this experience often, and I am sure that many of you can relate.

In personal therapy and my own journey of self-help discovery and growth, I learned a way to process intense anger or anxiety: I learned to tune in to my senses and pay attention to my surroundings. I focus on something I see, followed by something I can hear, smell, taste, and then touch. By the time I get through this task I've changed my focus and feel present and relaxed. When I played golf with Geshe-la for the first time and witnessed his gratitude and wonder for the beauty all around him, I realized I could apply this concept to my game of golf.

Believe me, the walk does not have to be spoiled because of a bad shot. It's always a good walk when you give yourself a chance to focus on the trees and the grass, the deer and the ripples across the water. I've learned to use my surroundings as a tool to manage the frustration of the imperfection of my skills in a round of golf, and so can you. Here's the way in which I process my anger and move on—maybe you can try something similar next time you find yourself overcome with anger.

After I hit the poor shot that is super costly to my score, I allow myself a moment of anger and might even bang my club on the ground or verbalize my frustration. I acknowledge my disappointment and anger at my error—there's nothing wrong with the emotion, but how we deal with it determines our further experience. I then take a deep, slow breath, look down the fairway and try to see the lay and flow of the hole, feel the direction of the wind, breathe in the smell of the trees and grass around me, and listen to the birds. Once I can feel my mind settle into my body again, I focus on the next shot. I see it finishing in my intended target zone in my mind's eye. As I walk into my setup, I pick a clear target, take the time to feel balanced in my feet and body, and swing with a connected focus to my target. When I walk down the fairway,

I make a concerted effort to not let my mind go back to the mistake made earlier; instead, I focus on the perfect cut of the grass, the friends playing with me, or the warm sun on my face. I enjoy the walk, and in doing so, do not attach the past mistake to my next shot or the rest of my round.

This does take practice, but if you consistently make an effort to acknowledge your feelings and then choose to put yourself back in charge of the present, you will reap great rewards. It's not about never being angry or disappointed ever again, but rather about feeling the anger and then putting yourself back in charge of your future.

I get to witness other people's self-destruction at the golf course every day. I see frustration build as players try repeatedly to hit shots in a direction they intend and fail more than half the time. They practice relentlessly and get frustrated and tired to the point of anger at themselves and the game. Many people feel that they can conquer their errors with sheer practice and determination and then get angry as their enjoyment of the game does not match their expectations.

Looking back at my career and listening to fellow golfers, I see that sometimes there's an effort to "conquer" golf, or anything you desire to be good at. This idea requires there to be a conqueror and a conquered. An angry golfer that leaves the course feeling disparaged, thinking about how to come back to the course to take vengeance—this is not a winner. I've found it less confrontational to think about learning to manage the game of golf and becoming better at playing the game *with* the golf course rather than against it. Together we can create the next shot, and

I can enjoy the course as a companion in my experience. In this way I can become a master of myself while I learn to become a master of my game.

Since my son was a baby, I've had a baby pacifier attached to my bag as a reminder, for when things do not go as planned, to take a moment to soothe myself and remember there are more important things to value in life. The thought of him and my family when I am on my golf walk often helps me stay centered and not get carried away by anger at my own imperfection or even the natural imperfections of the golf course.

Reflection

Do you get angry or frustrated on the golf course? How you deal with it can affect the rest of your game and the rest of your day.

Remember the last time you got angry on the course and how that felt in your gut. Now try to focus on your senses: Focus on something you see, then something you hear, smell, taste, and touch. Notice how you feel inside. At home, in your mind's eye, try to picture the beauty or sounds on the course, and then next time you play, practice bringing this awareness with you to help keep anger at bay or at least in its place.

15. Give-and-Take

More you give, more you get
Less you give, less you receive
That is the natural law of life
Include the bogeys you gave, the birdies you get
What you give will return in time

—Geshe-la

Geshe-la

I FIRST LEARNED about giving from my grandmother Darkyi and my birth mother, Namgyal Tso. These two ladies were very important in shaping my whole life.

When I was around five years old my mother passed away, but I still remember her always smiling at me and expressing her love for me. Even though I was so young, I was very conscious of her unconditional love; my memories are very certain of this. Later when I was a teenager, members of my family and others living in my village would tell me stories of my mother's kind and giving nature.

My grandmother lived until I was twelve and was also a very loving influence on my life. She taught me about the Tibetan saying *se chung gö*: Even a small amount of food can be shared. I learned to give food to everyone, even if there was only a little bit of it. This is a lesson that has always stayed with me.

I know there is a karmic law that the more you give, the more you will receive. Whatever good things we give, such as energy, will be returned to us. But my grandmother never talked about receiving—she just taught that we should be good people and help others. I learned the joy of giving food, a smile, love, or energy.

I don't assume I'll get everything I want in life. Instead, I tell myself that whatever the universe wants to give me, that's okay—that's what I'll get. I feel peace with that.

Even in my golfing journeys, I know that wherever the ball goes, that is the giving of the universe. I try to decide where it will go, but really, the universe chooses.

When we look around, we often see a culture with a survival mentality, focused on taking what is needed or what is wanted. People are often focused on what they need first, and when they give something away, it's often something they don't need or don't desire anymore. We all grew up thinking this way, but this is not really giving.

The concept that if you give you will receive in return is tricky. If your motivation to give is to receive, it may or may not work. Let's take, for example, a smile. When you want someone to smile at you, you smile at them first. Or when you want to speak with someone, you say "hello" first, wanting a reply or acknowledgment in return. But you have to know that you may wait in vain. This way, we learn that we must give first, without expectations, in order to receive.

Now I challenge you: What are you going to give? It's easy to give something you don't need or don't want anymore, but true giving is to share or give what you might need. If you want good health, happiness, compassion, kindness, understanding, or just to be heard, the best thing to give is just that. Lend someone an ear when they are troubled, be happy and share their joy when they are celebrating, assist someone in poor health, or reach out with a kind hand when someone needs help. This behavior is giving with positive intention and energy. To cultivate generosity or positivity you must sow it. This nature of being in the world has no expectation of receiving directly back, but just naturally creates a positive environment to exist for everyone around them.

You can apply this manner of being with everything you do. Try it on the golf course. With every shot you hit, give all your positive focus and intention to direct the ball to where you intend it to go with no pressure or expectation of what you get in return. When you are playing with other people, whether with them or competing against them, wish them only the best outcomes—birdies and good putts. You know how good it feels to get a birdie or to hole a long putt, so your intention is for them to experience that feeling as well. The true gift is the intention, not the actual thing one receives. We do not always receive what we want in life, no matter how good we try to be. In golf you will not always get a great result even though you practice extra hard. Golf will still give you bogeys even when your intentions are good, but when you work on giving positive intention, you will find you can work through the tough moments with greater ease. Maybe life or the course will even give you a shot in return when you least expect it.

Reflection

I notice that some players focus on what is going well, but others focus on what is going poorly. For some people, even if they hit a good shot, they focus on the negative. Where do you place your focus? Do you criticize yourself? Or do you think, "Could be worse, maybe next time I should try another way."

Jesse

THE GAME of golf is just like any activity in life—no matter what we do or play, there is a constant flow of energy. Energy is not created nor destroyed; it is only transferred, as we learned in physics in high school. If you can embrace this on the golf course when you play, it can enhance the fun of the game.

One of my very best rounds of golf was a casual practice round with my now wife, Nadine Ash, at Diamond Players Club in Clermont, Florida. I was having an amazing round where everything felt good and was going as planned. I was 10 under par on the fourteenth tee box, a par 3, about one hundred and ninety yards. I could feel a score of 59 brewing on this par-71 course, and I confidently pulled my six-iron out of my bag to play the tee shot. My swing was feeling pure. I had felt in control of every shot and this shot to the green felt just as perfect. The ball flew straight over the pin, landed on the green—and took a bounding leap off the back of the green.

I was flabbergasted by this change of fate. How could the perfect shot take such an unusual bounce on the greens I'd assumed I knew so well? The ball had been sitting so softly all day. I walked across the green, feeling the firmness under my feet, and carried my anger to the chip shot I faced behind the green. I flubbed my chip shot, which embarrassed and angered me more, and proceeded to make a double-bogey 5 on that hole. My perfect score of 59 was wiped away.

When all was going my way earlier in the round, I felt invincible and was indulging in the greatness that the game and course was giving me that day. Then, lo and behold, the round took an opportunity from me with one unpredictable bounce. It was like giving a child a bag of their favorite candy—and then taking away his favorite flavor. I was maddened by the inconsistency of the green condition and unable to enjoy finishing my great round with joy, because I felt cheated.

A short time after, I was able to reflect on the beauty of that round, and I can see that if I had just accepted the big bounce over the green as just a part of the course that day, I might have been able to save a par on that hole and have a 61 instead of the still-great score of 63 that I finished with.

Once I started to play the game as though against Old Man Par, as I shared earlier, I could see "tough breaks" as challenges played by the course to see if I could outperform him. The imperfections of the course, or the conditions, create an element of random unpredictability that challenges my resilience and creativity as a golfer. It is what makes this game intriguing. Sometimes you receive a lucky bounce that rewards you for an imperfect shot, and sometimes it takes your well-executed shot and sends it off course. We tend to accept the good things gladly and resent the bad breaks intensely. When I consider playing against Old Man Par, I envision laying down my best play and then seeing his response to my play. It's an exercise in give-and-take. Sometimes I give up a shot or two to his challenging play, and sometimes I take some shots from him with a few birdies made with good putts or an amazing, holed chip shot.

This gives the course a personality, and you can get caught up in the give-and-take of the game against your opponent, Old Man Par. This kind of imagination helps me stay focused even when my chips are down. If I play a wayward shot, or get an unfair bounce behind a tree, or my ball finds the only divot in the fairway, I focus on the challenge he has given me and try to hold my own by pulling off a great shot and recovering—or even better, winning a shot back when he least expects it. I see a lot of golfers who get frustrated at so-called bad bounces or errant shots that end up in tough situations. Their frustration leads to them giving away more shots to Old Man Par than they need to, sometimes continuing to the next hole. These players feel like the course took everything from them that day as they continue to give their energy to him even after the round, complaining about the course or their bad luck or inability to swing well that day.

If you can relate to the latter type of golfer, try to stay focused on playing this imaginary foe, or friend, and giving your best focus and positive energy to each shot or situation you find yourself in. You will find that you feel like you've taken shots back, or that you have minimized your losses and can focus on taking one or more back in the shots and holes that lie ahead.

Remember that energy is not lost; it is still there for you to exchange for something positive, so keep playing with it and be the best opponent you can be for Old Man Par. If he were super easy to beat, you wouldn't be hooked on playing this game. See him as a challenge on each shot, like playing a hand in a card game. Play the best shot you have available against what the course lays in front of you and enjoy the ride. This is more fulfilling and keeps you focused all the way to the end of the round—and through to the next round, as you cannot wait to see what you can do against him tomorrow. Sometimes the rollercoaster rounds of ups and downs, of give-and-take, make the best stories and memories. Remember his abilities or level of play changes with weather and setup conditions every day, just as yours do, depending on your feel or focus ability each day. If you have a handicap for your level of play, then playing to your handicap score would be your Old Man Par.

There is also something about having a constant, positive outflow of energy to your shots and the course. I notice while competing that on days I play well, I have an open flow of creativity and can see and complete the shots that are needed to play well. When I am protective and stop the outflow of energy, playing to avoid things instead of hitting positive targets, the course takes from me. It seems that the more fearfully I hold on to my energy, the more the course takes from me. On great days, it is the opposite. The more I give my energy free flow to focus on the positive targets, the more Old Man Par gives me. When your energy is flowing freely, it feels like you're creating your round and you're the master of the course, because you're open to working with what you're given. On days when you can only see the negative and are afraid of the obstacles he lays in front of you, he takes more from you and controls you, until you are depleted and exhausted.

The best way to try to get some consistency and purpose to your round every time you play is to accept Old Man Par as your opponent. With that imaginary opponent in mind, give your best positive energy and best positive focus on every shot all the way to the end, and enjoy the give-and-take along the way. This concept even allows you to enjoy the people you're playing with (or competing with) more, as you're focused on playing your personal best against your Old Man Par instead of them.

Some days you come out on top, and sometimes he wins, but either way it's a game that never ends. Enjoy the ride as a positive "give," and even when the course takes from you, see it as a positive challenge. Give humbly and graciously and he may return with a positive bounce or favorable lie.

Reflection

Think about your last round of golf. Do you remember some unfortunate bounces or rotten lies you got and how frustrated and unlucky it made you feel in that moment? Now imagine the golf course as a friendly opponent who, in those moments, one-upped you, and with whom you can laugh off the play and challenge back with a good recovery shot. Doesn't that make you feel lighter, and still in the game?

16. Balance and Tempo

Life can be perfect, if we can balance ourselves.

If we can reduce our obsessions, life can be balanced.

If we can manage our stress, life can be balanced.

If we can use wisdom and compassion together, life can be balanced.

If we can really slow down our habits of thinking and doing things, life can be balanced.

If we can focus and balance everything, life can be perfect.

—Geshe-la

Geshe-la

After I came to the West, I began teaching at universities and in different communities. At first it was very difficult. Every time, before I began to teach, I was overwhelmed with nervous energy. I was struggling with all the cultural and language differences between the East and the West, and this put me off balance. The methods, language, and vocabulary required to teach properly are very different in dissimilar cultures. Understanding questions was particularly difficult as I was sometimes unclear on the language. Slowly I learned that I must keep myself in balance in order to teach.

I remember one time teaching at Vancouver Island University. There were over seventy people in attendance, including many staff and teachers. Before I began, I told myself that I must be balanced in my energy: I would be focused and clear in understanding and answering questions. I was very aware of my language barrier in being a new English speaker and was very careful to clearly understand all questions. If I didn't understand the question, I would not answer it. I stayed in balance, and the teaching went very well. Now, I balance myself every time before I teach. Today, thanks to this experience, I'm comfortable with whoever is in front of me. My steady balance allows me to know who I am and that it's okay if people like me or not.

Everything should be balanced in life: Too much is not good, too little is not good.

One thing that affects our balance is our tempo. People tend to have a natural tempo based on their energy and ability. People with a slower tempo may be challenged in keeping pace. Or sometimes we may face challenges where our mind is rushing at an uncomfortable speed. When this happens, we must become aware of it and return to balance. Even after all this time, this can still be hard for me, but I do it every day. I am aware of my pace of movement, and I adjust my energy to accomplish what I can within a reasonable tempo of movement. I don't blindly follow my rushing mind.

Golfers often say "tempo" to themselves and others when they play as a reminder to swing not too fast and not too slow. This is easier said than done. Sometimes even when you remember before you start to swing, you forget on the backswing and then think "quickly" and a sense of urgency and forced energy takes over, and you mess up the shot.

It's very important to find your own natural tempo, both on and off the course. Do not let your mind pressure you to do something that's not right for you. When your energy is not balanced, it can affect your health, both mentally and physically. When you have good lifestyle management, things are balanced.

I've noticed that when I'm peaceful and balanced at home, with my family, my job, and in my community, I also feel balanced when I play golf. I hit balls well. I see the ball clearly. My swing is in balance: not too fast or too slow. I can focus on golfing and enjoying the company of my friends. But if I'm not balanced—in my stance, with my energy, or with my clubs—I'll have a bad result. It's all to do with the balance of energy. Everything is connecting and flowing, both in my physical body and in my mind.

How do we get in balance? We begin with our breath.

Start with being aware of your breathing patterns. Balance the inhale and exhale; don't inhale faster than you exhale, or exhale faster than you inhale. Breathe evenly.

Take time in the day to check in with your breathing rhythm. It takes practice to maintain awareness and make a change, but you'll be surprised how well your body will respond and accept the change when you give it good direction.

Breathing well helps us focus and relax. When your breath is balanced, your walking and talking start to balance, and you can choose better eating habits. You can become more focused and balanced at work. When you try to be balanced in everything you do, everything is affected immediately. It's all connected.

Be in balance mentally, physically, and financially. Be organized and purposeful with what you do. Tempo and balance go together. If you are in balance, then your tempo will be balanced too, and the journey will be smoother.

In golf, as well, our rhythm and tempo begin with the rhythm of our breathing. Balancing our breath helps us stay present, which keeps us in balance instead of allowing our forced or anxious energy to take control of the outcome of the shot at hand. It's like the saying, "To do more is to do less."

If I notice that my swing doesn't feel right, I try to rebalance myself immediately. I use a few different techniques; here are some you might try.

1. Mindfully breathe into your nose and out your mouth, from five to twenty-one times—twenty-one is a very auspicious number in my tradition.
2. Slowly recite a mantra in a whisper five to twenty-one times. Focusing on that will keep you balanced. I will often use the Bon five warrior seed syllable mantra and recite AH OM HUNG RAM DZA, but any focusing technique will help.
3. Check your body for tightness. Mindfully keep your shoulders down and relaxed. Be aware of your hands and relax any nerves or tightness in them.

BRINGING THE MIND HOME: LETTING GO

This is a good exercise to do before beginning any activity in which you need to focus. It can bring together our scattered minds as well as release tightness and stress in the body. Perform this exercise three to five times—if physically able to do so. It is an excellent practice before starting a game of golf. The purpose of this exercise is to relax and refresh body and mind. It is done while standing. The in-breath is taken while physically standing up tall and mentally bringing the mind and awareness home.

The out-breath is released in two bursts while physically bending over, doing two "bouncing" knee bends, and mentally letting go of all problems, worries, and attachments.

Here is the sequence in more detail:

To Start

As you take a long, deep breath, open your chest, and bending the elbows, lift your hands (turned down) up to shoulder height.

Exhale

Bounce 1: As you release the first breath, lean forward and bend the knees slightly as you drop down into the first down-and-up bounce. As you "hit the bottom" of the down part of the bounce, air is naturally forced out of the lungs. Feel the release and mentally say, "Letting go."

At the same time as you are dropping down, let your arms also drop down and swing to the back. You then naturally bounce up slightly, completing the first bounce. At this point you are still leaning over and the arms are extended behind you.

Bounce 2: Let the arms naturally swing forward just in front of you while your knees drop down into another bend and up again, blowing out more air at the bottom of that bend.

Inhale and Stretch

Inhale deeply as you stand up straight and continue to swing the extended arms up, over, and slightly behind your head. Mentally say, "Bringing the mind home."

If you can't stretch your arms up fully, just bring them back to the starting position, just in front of the shoulders.

Repeat

Now repeat the sequence, exhaling again while dropping the arms down and swinging them to the back while bouncing down and up on knees, as before, and returning to the full upright position.

Reflection

Sometimes I see people move very fast and they are very intense. You can notice when someone moves quickly versus in a more balanced way. Are they talking a lot or not too much? In Tibet we say we have eyes to see others, but we need a mirror to see ourselves and our own faults. How do you see yourself? It's easy to see qualities in others but you may not be able to see them in yourself. How would you describe your own balance and tempo?

Jesse

BALANCE AND TEMPO are two elements that go together in life no matter what we're doing or what sport we're playing. When we watch great athletes performing, we see their tremendous balance and innate rhythm, which help them succeed. We may not all have super athletic bodies, but we do have the ability to find our own balance and tempo, and the ability to train or live within a balance and tempo that are perfectly our own.

Nadine once told me the story of her first round as an LPGA Tour player back in 1998. It was her first tournament and was being held at Grand Cypress Resort in Orlando. Even though she was familiar with the course—this was her home city—she was very nervous and excited. Her college coach, Coach Pat Weis, was coming to watch, as a few ladies from her past teams were playing in the event. Nadine said she didn't play very well; she couldn't find her swing at all that day. She felt very off balance over the ball and could not find a rhythm. When Nadine was done with her round, Coach Weis came and told her that it looked like she was trying to hurry her play and get out of the other competitors' way. She said that she needed to slow down and take her earned space in the event. Nadine told me she knew what her coach meant but had a difficult time finding that comfort zone of relaxed space that year on tour. Nadine even told me that later that year her sponsor mentioned to her that she looked uncomfortable and suggested she think of her game as a dance; once she felt the rhythm of that dance: telling her, her game would flow with more ease. Great advice, but as I am sure many of you readers can relate, when you feel stressed, following advice can be easier said than done.

A couple of years later, Nadine and I had met, and we would practice our golf together. I was very comfortable with my putting, which I still consider to be the strength of my game. Sometimes, to work on my putting, I would use a metronome to feel and ingrain a comfortable rhythm with my putting routine and stroke. We experimented with different rhythm beats for Nadine, and it was interesting to see the mixed pace of her setup routine and putting stroke. She would do her setup routine comfortably but then stand over her putt for a long time with a long, slow stroke. Once we noticed this hesitancy and break in flow of her putting process, she started to commit to a rhythm that was consistent from beginning to end. We also started to experiment with matching the metronome beat to our walking pace. We noticed a comfortable rhythm that was personal to each of us.

This experimental adventure with the metronome was fundamental to us realizing a personal, comfortable beat to our existence—a rhythm we generally walk and talk to, so to speak. It dawned on Nadine that this was her natural dance step, which was relaxing and helped her find her balance. The rhythm of her dance around the course! Now when we play golf, we're aware of getting ourselves into our comfort rhythm, starting with our walking pace, swing pace, and setup routines. One of my best friends once advised me to take walks more often, especially when stressed out or needing to figure something out in my head. I now realize that when we walk for a while, we tend to fall into a comfortable tempo to our step and it feels balanced, and we tend to think better when this happens.

Why not try this for your own golf game? The way to start establishing a rhythm is to first pay attention to your breathing. Listen to its pattern. Does it seem fast or a little mixed up? If so, start to count on the inhale (to four, for example) and again on the exhale to the same count. This will slow down your thoughts and you'll start to feel relaxed. Find an equal inhale and exhale count that feels effortless to you. Now your breathing is balanced and has a tempo that is comfortable to you.

Next, take a walk. When you are walking feel the rhythm of your footsteps. When we rush around, we don't pay attention to this rhythm, and when we're stressed and distracted by hurrying, we often trip over things or our own feet. When you focus on the beat of your feet, walking can be meditational, and the rhythm can bring balance to you, physically and mentally. Try different paces of walking, and pay attention to which tempo feels the most comfortable to you. When you're familiar with your own rhythm, it's easier to notice when you're out of sorts or off balance, and easier to find your way back to your personal balance. Finding your tempo and balance of breathing and walking are great ways to begin getting ready for a round of golf.

Once you've found a comfort zone with a walking pace, you can practice paying attention to your shot routine tempo and your swing tempo. Get a metronome, even as an app on your phone, and experiment with different beat speeds to find your own natural rhythm that works best for you. Once you've learned your comfort pace, then the game of golf starts to feel like a dance and the rhythm becomes relaxing and has a mantra-like ability to help you focus. You'll find that when you can match your personal pace, your balance gets better too.

You can also practice physical balance with your golf swing on the driving range. This kind of practice can actually help you find better tempo, as well, if you're feeling out of sorts. I encourage my students to spend time swinging a club with their feet together, with their bodyweight evenly balanced on both feet. When hitting a few balls this way with a wedge, you quickly become aware of your balance. Then, if you can, stand on your left leg, with only your right toes lightly touching the ground for stability. Swing your wedge, staying balanced on your left leg all the way to your finish. When you get good at this, you'll feel like you allow gravity to help your swing accelerate through the ball, and you'll start to find a natural rhythm with your balance. You'll also notice that as your physical balance improves, your tempo will get better too.

It's also possible to practice tempo on the driving range. I was fortunate enough to be able to work on my game with Charlie King, a PGA golf instructor who wrote the books *You're Not Lifting Your Head* and *Golf's Red Zone Challenge*. He used to make me hit shots on the range with varying swing speeds. I would hit a nine-iron with a full-length swing but only 20 percent of my maximum swing speed; I'd hit the next ball at 40 percent, then 60 percent, then 80 percent, and then 100 percent, as fast as I could. Then I would work my way back down. It put me in control of how hard I wanted to hit the ball while still having a balanced and rhythmic swing. Many golfers I teach can only swing at maximum speed, with a haphazard hit-and-hope golf swing. They find it difficult to gain control at slower speeds. Increasing swing speed in stages is a great drill to practice tempo.

Another way to practice rhythm and tempo is pitching from twenty up to one hundred yards. Take your pitching or approach wedge, and practice hitting the ball to targets set at twenty, forty, sixty, eighty, and one hundred yards, and then back down again. This is incredibly beneficial for your scoring shots as well as a very relaxing drill that helps you fall into a tempo with your swing.

Balance and tempo go hand in hand. When you start to try the activities mentioned above, that will become very clear. The trick, once you have found your own balance and beat, is to stay within them no matter who you are playing golf with. Some golfers play extremely fast, and it can seem like their goal is to get off the course as quickly as possible. Others are quite the opposite, with an extremely time-consuming shot process and slow game. Once you find a routine and walk that are comfortable to operate in, own them and commit to them. If your group is behind in time, don't give up your rhythm and balance to accommodate; instead, find areas of your game in which to be more efficient, like being prepared to play your shot when it is your turn and leaving your golf equipment on the side of the green you'll exit from before you putt. These efficient choices are part of the etiquette of the game and can be learned, but there's no need to give up your rhythm and balance. If someone plays superfast, keep your rhythm and balance. Do not change to accommodate their frustration. If you're off balance, your score will be higher and your game slower. You manage your pace; it's up to them to manage their own game.

When we organize our time efficiently in life, we feel more competent and confident with everything we do. When we have a clear purpose to our action, we feel more balanced and less likely to feel thrown off by surprises in our path. Learn to be aware of your tempo and balance in life in general, and you'll be able to manage your stress and your ability to perform under stress. Focus on balance physically and mentally, and then find your own rhythm that gives you a beat that relaxes you and helps you reach your potential—in golf and in life.

Reflection

Sometimes when you feel out of balance it helps to go to extremes. The next time you go to the course, and you feel sluggish and slow, or even hurried and stressed, feel the rhythm of your feet and walk as fast as you can and then walk really slowly, and then see if you can walk in a more comfortable rhythm. It will help you find your natural pace. You can do this with your golf swing too—swing a few practice shots really fast and then swing really slowly for a few shots. Then you may feel more comfortable at your regular pace again.

17. The Master

The moment you get to the course
You start searching for the master
You can be your own master; find this master
A pro can be your master,
A body swing can be your master
Your clear awareness can be your master
Your true nature can be your master
Let golf be the method of connection

—Geshe-la

Geshe-la

THERE ARE TWO ways to become a master of any kind of skill. The first is that we're naturally endowed with a talent for mastering a certain endeavor, such as music, sports, engineering, or spiritual leadership, without having to work too hard. It's my belief that this sort of ability is karmic. The second way to become a master requires lots of effort, learning, and practice. This way requires the right environment and encouragement, like support from family and friends, and a teacher who is themselves a master.

In my tradition, when we talk about a "master," we're talking about a spiritual master, like a meditation master. His Holiness Menri Trizin Rinpoche was the previous high master of the ancient Bon tradition of Tibet and the thirty-third lineage holder of the tradition. Several years ago, I was able to participate in and help organize the retreat when he was teaching in San Francisco. During this retreat, he spoke about the concept of "master" and what it really means.

There are three levels of master. We call them the *outer master*, the *inner master*, and the *secret master*. The outer master is the one who has become proficient in whatever skill or spiritual practice you're trying to perfect. This master is the one who has the experience, the knowledge, or the wisdom you need; they can give you instruction on the skill you are trying to master, and they can give you direction, guiding you to know your inner master as yourself.

Your inner master is your self-awareness, which you use as your guide, learning from it where you are on your journey and what needs more work. You learn through your senses, which in Bon Buddhism are understood to be seeing, hearing, smelling, tasting, feeling, and thinking. For instance, be aware of seeing how the ball is placed on the fairway, feel the tension in your body and how you are gripping the club, and think about the process of hitting the ball. Then mindfully relax and swing. By being mindful of the senses, instead of letting yourself wander into the objects of the senses and become distracted, you are connected to your inner master.

The secret master is what we call the primordial awareness, or your true nature of mind, your authentic self. It is that gut instinct that leads you when you pay attention to your inner self. That is your secret master. In Tibetan Bon Buddhism your secret master is your natural mind. The natural mind is always pure and perfect, even though we are blocked from seeing it by our ignorance and lack of awareness. Yet the natural mind is always there, behind our ignorance and lack of seeing. We can recognize it when we're relaxed and know that we have prepared as much as we can by learning from the outer and inner masters and can now let go of our ego-centered worries. We can relax and accept everything that comes our way. We are able to respond naturally to changing conditions. We just decide what is good to do next. Some people may recognize this as being in a state of flow. This is your secret master. It is perfect, as always.

A flow state, also known as "being in the zone," is the mental state in which a person performing an activity is fully immersed in a feeling of energized focus, full involvement, and enjoyment in the process of the activity. In essence, flow is characterized by the complete absorption in what one does. Nothing is disturbing the mind. In Tibetan, the word *lhundrup* is used to describe behavior that is spontaneous, without effort, and feels natural and connected. This is the secret master.

In the case of golf, the outer master is the teaching pro. The inner master is your awareness of your swing. Knowing your secret master is to feel complete joy and compassion for yourself, allowing you to discover all the good qualities within yourself that were hidden until you learned to see them. Most people just want to hit a good shot and don't connect to the swing, the inner master. They may know the inner master intellectually but have not yet mastered the knowledge. The inner master is where your lessons are internalized, allowing you to understand what the correct swing feels like and to visualize clearly where you want the ball to go. You are mindful and can remember what you were taught. You know how to respond to the conditions and environment around you. The inner master understands and can implement the skills taught by the outer master. Your swing reflects your mind. It becomes free and relaxed when connected to the secret master.

Each of these three masters is necessary to truly master anything. First, you need the outer master, who can introduce you to your inner master, which is your own mind, your awareness. The inner master is necessary to introduce you to your secret master. Once the outer master has introduced the inner master, who introduces you to your secret master, they all become unified. They become one and then there is no difference between them. The whole purpose is to discover and connect to the secret master though the outer and inner masters.

The three levels are important and necessary for both your spiritual journey and your sports journey. They depend on each other. People think the master is only the outer master and do not realize that they need to grow to be their own master. They have not yet realized that they can develop their inner master and secret master to connect with the outer master for a complete experience.

Earlier I shared a saying from Tibet: "You have the eyes to see others, but you need a mirror to see yourself." Your mirror is the outer master, who can reflect back to you the other masters. Once you see them for yourself, they become more accessible to you. When you find all three, you become perfected. Your kindness or skills show. Whether you are on a golf journey or a spiritual journey, you reach your final destination.

Reflection

What is the master for you? Are you the master or not?

Each person has their own unique talents: Some may be a master of golf; some may be a master of something else. What is your unique talent? How do you use it? Do you use the master? Are you continuously developing your relationship with the master?

Jesse

TO BECOME a master at anything requires time, knowledge, dedication, and practice. To play golf is to be inundated with information on the golf swing by lots of enthusiastic students of the game, but as a golf professional, I see lots of confusion and frustration on what information is good to follow. I have been one of those eager students of the game my whole career and have been on a search for swing information that gives me a clear and complete understanding of the mechanics and science of the swing. Now, I finally feel that I have that; I feel like I am now a master of my golf game every time I go out there. Not because my swing or my round is perfect every time, but because I understand what I'm focused on doing and because I feel like I can make good decisions on what shot to play and how to execute it. But how did I get there?

I started playing golf in my late teens at Camrose Golf Course, in Camrose, Alberta. My mom would drop me off at the course after school and I would hit balls and play, and I also had a part-time job with the local pro, Bill Goldsworthy. Bill would help me out with the basics of the golf swing and taught me the entry-level tools of the golf trade. He called me "Pro" every day. It was here that my love of the game began.

As a young man finishing high school, I decided that I wanted to be a golf professional. My family sent me to the Golf Academy of the South, in Florida, to study for a diploma in Golf Complex Management. I also became a keen student of the game itself. I had an event at the end of my studies in which I needed to play under a certain score to achieve my PGA status. This playing test was called a Player Ability Test. During this time, I worked with two PGA of America professionals: Charlie King and Al Flashner. Charlie taught me a lot about shaping and creating shots and mastering rhythm; I've mentioned his name in some of the other chapters in this book.

I returned to Canada in 1998 and continued my education at Camosun College in Victoria, British Columbia. After graduating I began my teaching career as a golf instructor, where I learned to listen, communicate, and formulate my own thoughts and theories of how to swing a golf club efficiently and play the game well. There is nothing like teaching someone else to help you integrate the information other masters have provided you along your journey and form your own concepts. While I taught golf and worked as a PGA of Canada professional, I also worked hard on my swing mechanics and my short game, and as I did, I started to learn my personal style, the strengths and weaknesses of my own game. Every year I would save some money I earned in the summer in Canada and head south to Orlando, Florida, for the winter, where I would work on my game with PGA Master Professional Carl Rabito. I absorbed everything I could from him, and it was through practicing with him that I met Nadine, who was working with Carl at the same time. We spent hours discussing swing theories and comparing notes from our past instructors of the game.

We both had been blessed with teachings from many different masters that each taught us something valuable and helped us discover abilities or traits within ourselves. Nadine has a long list of masters and inspirations along her life and golf journey; in addition to Carl, she worked with renowned golf instructors like Mike Adams, Chuck Cook, Dick Harmon, and Fred Griffin. Together we had compiled a huge file of valuable information.

Over the years, we deciphered the knowledge and created our own definition of the golf swing and the game that we learned best suited our own needs. It was such an exciting time to realize our wealth of experience and knowledge and apply it to ourselves—and then return to Canada together and share this with so many new students of our own. I created a training aide called the Right Touch; Nadine and I developed the patent together. It was in these discussions and writing exercises that we got to explore ideas, question past theories, and really formulate our own understanding.

Nadine and I were able to then help each other become masters of our own game by discussing weaknesses and strengths and researching methods and theories to continue our path to be better players and teachers of the game. To this day, I still reach out to other masters sometimes—such as Mike Bender and my fellow PGA of Canada professional on Vancouver Island John Randal—and always will. A fresh set of professional eyes on your game is very helpful when you feel stuck or confused. Sometimes we are too close to the forest to see the trees, and a new master can give a fresh perspective.

All these wonderful instructors are all masters that

came into my golf world and my life at certain times to help me grow as a player, teacher, and human being. Each one taught me something new and created more discussion and learning. Just when I thought I had a strong mastery of my golf skills, my eyes were opened again when I met my friend, fellow author, and spiritual master Geshe-la. He opened my mind and my heart to becoming a spiritual master for myself on and off the golf course. Our discussions led to the chapters in this book and to the growth of my potential as an instructor and master to my students of the game. He brought awareness to bad habits that could be challenged with more mindful, positive actions and perspectives, and he brought awareness to the masterful thoughts and habits I already had, so that I could now express and share with others more effectively.

I have learned over time that there are many masters around us to learn from, and we have an active responsibility to reach out to them when we are ready to learn. It is the relationships with these teachers along your journey that help you eventually help yourself and become your own master at your own golf game or in life.

As a student of the game, it's important to find an instructor you trust and have a good, consistent rapport with, a master to teach you and help you become self-aware on your journey to becoming your own master. Lots of golfers watch and try to learn from the abundant information online, but I find this leads to more misunderstanding and misplaced effort; it doesn't relate to them directly and there is no back-and-forth flow of energy and information to allow for personal growth for the player or the master. As you start to understand your own golf swing and have a clear path of growth with a teacher, you can set goals, see progress, and start becoming your own master over time. You'll notice that I had many teachers of the game; some of those changes were due to moving and some were because I'd reached a block in my progress and looked for a new perspective to reach another level. Some professionals find it helpful to have different masters for different parts of their game, like a swing coach and a short-game coach. And even these might change if the player feels stuck.

To be the master of your game requires knowledge, clarity, and acceptance. Just because you know how to swing your club does not mean you will perform with perfection—but it gives you more confidence, the ability to plan how to achieve your goals, and more defined focus over each shot. Having a clear understanding of yourself and the mechanics you are performing leads to less frustration when you hit a poor shot or are in a challenging situation, because you have the tools to make choices and can do something different next time. Having a teacher on your journey gives you a sounding board and someone to help you keep refining your learning path and goals.

I like to think of the instructor, or your master, as a reflection of you. They are communicating to you what they see from you and thus reflect back an image or idea that they would like you to then reflect back to them for improvement. One of the flaws that ails my swing is losing the starting posture of my right leg on my backswing. The instructor makes me aware of the swing flaw and finds a way to help me feel aware of the difference to then enable me to make the change. It's a beautiful flow of respect and information suffused with energy and trust. If there comes a time when this flow seems to get blocked with frustration, then it may be time for a good conversation; if the problem remains unsolved it might be time to consider a fresh pair of eyes and new communication style.

Choose your master to learn from. It is smart to research your instructor or ask for some time to ask them questions about their golf theories or knowledge. This will also give you a chance to see if your communication styles suit each other. I enjoy it when a student of the game comes to ask me such things, as I get to know them better and understand their goals and knowledge of the game too.

Remember that to become a master of your game, you need to manage yourself and your growth effectively. This includes finding a compatible teacher for the level you are at and developing a plan with that master to improve your game and become your own master on the course. It also includes behaving like a teacher, which is to have patience, attention, understanding, acceptance, and focus, as well as confidence and commitment to a plan.

Sometimes a master might meet you just for a moment but nevertheless say something that has a profound effect on the way you think about something. It could be a family member or a fellow golfer. As I previously mentioned, Ken Harrelson told once me to treat my golf ball with care. That statement changed my perspective on how I saw my golf ball and my thought processes over every shot I played from then on. He was a master in that moment.

Finding your own master is such an intriguing and rewarding journey. I know you'll also enjoy the connections and conversations you have along the way with teachers and friends on that same path.

Reflection

Take a moment to think about a person in your life that inspired a change in you in some way. It could've been a friend, a family member, a schoolteacher, an employer, or a work companion. Sometimes the master shows up for a moment to teach us something, and sometimes we actively search for someone with the skills to help us develop into our own master.

If you're reading this book, then you're most likely trying to improve your game, so put yourself in the driver's seat; find your own master/instructor so that you can educate yourself on your own game, and so you can be your own master to get back on track if things go wayward on the course. Find a master that will help you be the best version of you.

18. Power of Three

May strength and balance enable my body
to perform.
May my mind be free from the prison of
perfection so I can create.
May my spirit relax in acceptance of the
challenges that come.

—Jesse

Geshe-la

I FIRST MET JESSE in 2020 at a golf club where he worked as a pro. One day, while I was practicing on the range, I saw him teaching someone. I also noticed he was watching my swing. After his lesson was over, he came over to me and watched me practice. He even brought a chair and sat down. I was very nervous being watched; I'd never had lessons before. He knew nothing about me personally, but he commented that I had a good swing and then gave me some tips on how to improve. I was very grateful for his advice and that no payment was asked for. He introduced me to Nadine, who also worked in the pro shop.

I eventually did start taking lessons with Jesse, and as I began to get to know him, I found him to be very open about who he is. He told many stories about his life journey, and one story he shared was about his belief in the power of number three and the triangle. He believes everything is connected to the number three. At first, I didn't really understand his point of view, but as I considered what he said, I realized that three is an auspicious number according to my tradition. Many Bon teachings are categorized into threes. There are three dimensions to the universe: the upper (god) realm, the middle (human) realm, and the lower (*naga*, or water spirit) realm.

There are also three capacities of consciousness: higher, middle, and lower. The nature of self is organized into threes as well: There is the outer self, which is our physical body; our inner self, which is our energy and sense of self; and our most-inner self, the secret level, the consciousness or nature of mind that is who we really are.

Many stories even say that to accomplish something, give it at least three tries. For instance, the Buddha's cousin Ananda had to ask him three times to ordain his aunt as the first Buddhist nun.

The more Jesse and I talked about the number three, the more I realized that it can be an important framework to help us change our perceptions and our lives in a helpful and practical way.

For instance, in Bon Buddhism, we talk about the three doors, or *go sum*: the body, speech, and mind. The body refers to your actions, speech refers to the words you use, and the mind is your intention. We use these three doors to create positive or negative intentions, actions, and speech. If you want positive consequences, then create positive output from those three doors. If you want negative consequences, then use them for negative output. Therefore, in order to transform yourself or your life, your goal would be to be mindful of what you say, mindful of how you act, and mindful of your thoughts. These are the three doors through which we create our own karma.

Then there are the three wisdoms: listening, contemplation, and meditation. On a spiritual journey, in order to gain wisdom, the first thing you must do is listen. People are often quick to speak their opinion but don't make listening a priority. We have two ears and one mouth: We should listen more than we speak. Then we need contemplation. It's important to contemplate when you learn something, whether it's through pain and suffering or even through happiness. Whatever you're feeling or going through should be met with contemplation, so that you can process emotions and consider how to move forward. That's the way of wisdom of contemplation. *Meditation* means deep concentration, or mindfulness of and focus on what you've learned through contemplation. Without listening, there is no contemplation, and without contemplation there's no meditation. Those are three important steps we try to work through for everyday life. If you're working on transforming yourself, these are three valuable wisdoms.

Then there are also three root sufferings. Where does suffering come from? The causes of our suffering are ignorance, anger, and attachment. Every thought we have is connected to a feeling, so there are eighty-four thousand emotions that we have every day. Those emotions and thoughts are created or rooted in these three root emotions of ignorance, anger, and attachment. In order to become free from suffering we need to become free from those three root emotions. To free ourselves of these emotions, it is important to be aware of how we use our three doors and to be mindful of developing the three wisdoms.

You can see that all of this can be practiced every day and even on the golf course. It's important to focus on the positive to create positive results when you play, for yourself and those you play golf with. The three wisdoms are important for learning the game and creating mindful change and growth.

Reflection

Tibetans believe that the numbers three, five, and eight are auspicious. Do you have any auspicious numbers? What are they? What does it mean, to you, that they are auspicious?

Jesse

I NOTICE SYSTEMS of three a lot in my life and often wonder if others notice them too. The old saying "Everything happens in threes" often refers to a run of bad luck, but I think it can be seen in many areas of life. For instance, did you grow up with the idea of an angel on one shoulder and the devil on the other? It's always given me the image of a pair of polar opposites with me in the middle; there it is, the power of three—the angel, the devil, and me. We also speak of "me, myself, and I": the battle over heart, mind, and ego.

In my many business relationships in life, in situations when I was trying to prove my worth or to get my point across with meaningful impact, I always felt like I was in a fight, like I was always pushing against the universe. Then one day, several years ago, I was discussing ancient symbols with my wife and son, and I felt a sudden connection to the infinity symbol. I developed my own interpretation of this symbol, linking it to energy that flows constantly back and forth. I had an epiphany that all of my business dealings were like a negotiation around the infinity sign. I could see the "power of three" in this so clearly. There was always me on one side of the dilemma pulling and pushing energy and the other person pulling or pushing on the other side. Somewhere along that infinity symbol the transaction would finish, often with someone feeling like the victor and the other like the defeated. I suddenly could see that if the two sides negotiating could be brought to the center, relations would feel less aggressive and selfish and more symbiotic. For me it was an "Aha" moment and I started to see the power of three everywhere. There are always the two sides negotiating and the deal needing to get finalized. I had a fresh way to approach life and people, and I have enjoyed the journey far more since my new vision on the world.

Now, no matter the situation, I create an awareness of both sides, and instead of feeling like I'm fighting to prove a point, I calmly consider what the other side needs in order to meet me in the middle. I have found that just by thinking this way in a stressful circumstance, the energy I send is calmer and more inviting to discussion, and this affects the demeanor of the negotiating party as well. The balanced, peaceful center is a far superior place to create positive relations.

I have even used my personal epiphany on the golf course. On the golf course there is the player, the target, and the negotiation on the type of shot to be played for an acceptable outcome. For example: A player wants to set themselves up for a birdie on a par 5. They find themselves in the middle of the fairway at a distance from the green that they might be able to make with a great shot. The target is the flag set in the back right portion of the green, which is protected in front by a pond extending across the fairway and about twenty yards wide. The negotiation starts to happen—the player feels good after hitting a good drive and is buzzing at the idea of getting a birdie on this hole. If they could hit the green with their second shot, a birdie would only be two putts away. The target then shows its side of the bargain—the flag is right at the back of the green with the flag stick bending in the wind, blowing straight at the player's face. The reeds in the pond are leaning in the wind back in the player's direction. If the player chooses to go with ego and beat the course at its own game, they're forcing energy in one direction, and the course with wind, hazard, and back-pin placement is fighting back in the other direction. I, the player, now see this as a negotiation between the will of both sides. I sense the warning of the course with the signals it's showing me, and I know I would like to get a birdie, but maybe there's a better way to achieve it. I respect the energy of the target and still give myself the best opportunity to produce my best score on the hole. I relax my aggressive energy and play a shot short of the pond in a place to give myself my favorite-length wedge shot to that back-pin placement. The energy for that situation is calmer. We reach an agreement that the target and I agree with, and I can play the hole out, giving myself the best opportunity to make a birdie—and if not, a very solid par.

When I approach my golf shots this way, I see it as a negotiation with the intention of finding balance and peace in the outcome. I see many golfers trying to force their will on the golf course and then coming off feeling very defeated. Think back for a second on my infinity symbol idea. These players are forcing energy, demanding, and getting angry at the negative results. Their energy is constantly trying to flow to the outer sides of the loops, when the peace is in the center of the negotiation.

This is just one example of how I use the power of three

to play golf, but there are many groups of three present in the game. There are par 3s, par 4s, and par 5s. There are usually three types of flags or pin positions on the greens: one at the back, the middle, and the front. You've got your hook, your slice, and your straight shot. There is your ball, your club, and yourself, the player. And the game itself is a simple interaction of you, Old Man Par, and the result on the scorecard. You can see how you can walk your way around the golf course organizing your thought process according to the power of three.

Nadine uses a simple mantra given to her by her mum, who didn't golf but who used to watch her play. Her mum said, "Nadine, it's easy. Just think 'Down the middle, on the green, and in the hole.'" This simple observation of golf as a three-step process by a non-golfer became a concrete focus in Nadine's competitive approach to the game. I adopted it too, and I find it a useful mantra to ground myself when things start to go a little awry; it helps me slow down the mind and set up a rhythm to the round. Get the tee shot forward down the fairway, focus on getting the next shot to the green or as close as you can, and then focus on completing the hole by getting the ball into the hole. It's as easy as one, two, three.

Even when you're focused on the shot at hand, you can break down your decision into right side, left side, or straight. Is the flag at the back, middle, or front? When you analyze your shot, you look at whether it was a fade, a draw, or a straight shot. Even when you read a putt on the green, you pay attention to speed, break, and incline. When I can break down the activity into clear parts, I can take decisive action on clear details and have complete acceptance of the result.

I use this concept in my golf game and life to help me process circumstances and create the best result I can. It helps me have greater awareness, a broader understanding of circumstances, and a more mindful approach to any situation. I have discovered that instead of fighting the forces from opposing sides of the flow of energy, I can instead find a balanced center where the energy converges for an optimal result.

When you go for your next round of golf, I suggest you first try the concept of "Down the middle, on the green, and in the hole." It's a very relaxing thought and the three-step process will help you stay focused on the shot at hand.

Once this becomes a comfortable habit to the rhythm of your game, try to see if you can get into the negotiating idea, where you, the player, are negotiating the best deal with the golf course to produce the best result. This will help you nurture the habit of being present and acknowledging the details of the conditions presented by both sides in order to create your optimal result and balance your game.

Reflection

Think about how you feel when you play golf. Do you sometimes feel overwhelmed by the struggle or even sometimes ego-pumped by victory? Maybe you're plagued by doubt on one shoulder and your will on the other, and you feel stuck in the middle, trying to negotiate a decent round of golf. Consider negotiating each shot with the target, by contemplating the circumstances the course is presenting, and come to a decision that feels balanced, centered, and positive. Bite-size challenges. It's as easy as one, two, three!

19. Rejuvenate the Energy

Sleep more, stress less.

Focus more, think less.

Exercise more, be less restless.

Save more energy, waste less time.

When you rejuvenate your energy, your feeling and ability will be very different.

—Geshe-la

Geshe-la

IN 1997 I WAS LIVING in Dharamshala, India, writing and editing my books that were published in the Tibetan language. I was living in Upper Dharamshala and working in Lower Dharamshala; it took about an hour to go back and forth each day. Every day I sat staring at a computer and working with others who were helping me edit. Before this I'd been focused on my personal practice, and I soon found this new routine to be very exhausting. I felt myself getting weaker and I lost weight. I was very stressed mentally and energetically; I was nervous working with those who were helping me. My energy became very low, which created mental, physical, and spiritual problems. I felt things were falling apart, but I was able to finish my work. After I finished, I realized the impact that too much stress and intensity had on my well-being. Then I committed myself to refocus on saving my energy and managing my stress level through the practice of meditation and awareness.

Much later, in Canada, I was watching the golf channel and listened as a doctor talked about the importance of rejuvenating our energy. He pointed out that sleep, meditation, and food can all be effective in stress management. Without finding an energetic balance in our lives, we may not accomplish what we want.

I've since noticed that it shows in my golf game whether I've had enough sleep and am energetically balanced before I play. Better energy balance equals better game.

It is very important to protect and develop your energy. Our life runs on energy, and yet people don't often focus on it, or maybe they don't even believe in energy. They focus on physical or emotional issues without realizing what their energy (or lack thereof) is doing to them or the quality of their lives.

Time can be linked to your energy as well. You should protect your time. Don't waste it doing things that do not refill your cup. Be thoughtful about how you spend your time with people. Do not waste time on the internet or partying. Spend your time and energy on what is important to you. Focus your energy on your health, on being at peace, or on activities that bring you happiness and accomplishment. When you spend time and energy on this type of focus, then you feel rejuvenated and fulfilled. Creating positive energy for yourself and others around you creates more energy that returns to you. Activities that do not send positive energy into the world tend to take away from your cup and leave you feeling tired and exhausted. Sometimes the grind of work or responsibilities can take all our energy, and we need to take time to reenergize to stay healthy and happy.

Sometimes even when we do things that we enjoy, we're too tired to allow them to be rejuvenating. One big problem for some is lack of quality sleep due to stress or partying or too many jobs. Even enjoying a game of golf can be difficult without a good night's rest. When you play golf, if your energy is low, you cannot focus, and your balance is off physically and emotionally.

I know that when I get a good rest the night before I play golf, my energy is high, and I feel stronger and more balanced physically and mentally and am better able to go the distance for a full round. Sleep and meditation are two of the most effective ways to rejuvenate and balance your energy. One meditation technique is to be fully present and aware of what is around you. Be aware of your feelings: Are you tired, tense, or nervous? Be fully aware of the sounds around you, not just absently noting what you hear but with full awareness: Are you hearing birds, wind, people, or your own footsteps? Say to yourself, "I am fully aware of what I am hearing." Do the same with taste and smell and be aware of what your body is experiencing. Accept it all without judgment.

Another practice I use to achieve the same result is to meditate on the stillness of my body. This can be done sitting or standing. While being still I ground every part of my body: hands, feet, shoulders, etc. I bring my awareness to my senses and the stillness of my body. My breathing is soft and balanced. My energy balances. I am still, like a giant Buddha statue or a mountain no wind can disturb.

Sometimes when I find myself becoming obsessed with my game or score, I will consciously decide to focus on five different objects around me. I am careful to look without judgment, whether it's at a face, water, or my club. For example, I will mindfully look at a tree and be consciously aware of what I am looking at. Slowing down, being present and aware, shifts your mind and you naturally become more relaxed. Your thinking changes, your feelings change, your energy changes, and the game becomes easier. Rejuvenating and conserving energy is important to our well-being. Protect your sleep, and take time to rest. Do exercise that brings you more balance, physically and mentally. Investing time in ways to rejuvenate energy builds a healthy body and mind, which brings quality to all of our activities, interactions, and lives.

Reflection

What is the difference in your energy level before and after a game? How do you feel walking onto the course? What do you feel when you're packing your clubs back into your car?

Personally, I'm always excited before a game; I'm like a dog wanting to play with a ball. Afterward I may feel calm, pleasantly tired, and ready for home. Or I may still have energy and want to hit more balls.

Do you sleep better after a day of golf? How do you sleep the night before? Is there less sleep because you're excited?

Jesse

I THINK EVERYONE is looking for rejuvenation on a regular basis. People are tired—tired of work, of stress, or of the normal routine of their day. We look for fun activities, or try to create relaxation time, to rejuvenate our energy and zest for life. Lots of people choose to play golf to rejuvenate their energy as a break from their routine. This is a great idea as it gets you outside, walking and talking with friends. Unfortunately, I often see golf suck the life and energy out of people if they are focused on the wrong part of the game.

Everyone is excited to be at the course, whether it is for the walk, the friends, or the chance to beat their best score, but I see players get deflated and defeated by their score even as early as the first hole. When playing golf, it's routine to write your score or those of your playing partners at the end of each hole, so it is difficult to keep the focus on your score from controlling the energy of your game. When players start their round well, they're energized and excited to keep it going. When they have a high score on a hole, it can drag their energy down and they carry the defeat to the next hole. The game becomes heavy and exhausting instead of rejuvenating. If you choose golf as an activity to rejuvenate your energy, I advise you to not let your score be the engine that creates the energy, or it will be a turbulent ride. Attaching your enjoyment to the overall result or score of an activity can take away the enjoyment of the activity itself.

When I play golf, I'm energized by the ability to create a new shot every time I hit the ball. The chance of hitting an awesome shot each time gives me the excitement of opportunity through the entire course, to the point that I wish there were more holes to play at the end of my round. I see each shot as its own entity. Each shot is a creative task with a beginning and an end, and my goal is to create something amazing with each one. With this mindset, the whole round fills me with the energy of possibility. This is how I rejuvenate my energy by playing golf after a long day at work.

I learned a lot about energy rejuvenation on Orange Tree Golf Club one day in Orlando. I was playing a friendly game with some people I knew, but it was a pretty muted round, with everyone, including me, focused on our own games. We were toiling away in our own world, focused on our own interests. When I think back, this was par for the course when us young pros got together to play a round. Late into the back nine, one of the young men hit an errant tee shot with an iron on a par 3. It went off to the right and just as he was about to dismiss it as a disappointing shot, it was as if the tree that was about to swallow it created a backstop and threw his rejected ball toward the hole, like a professional outfielder. We were all shaken out of our spiritless state, and we cheered as the ball careened onto the green and began its roll toward the hole. This dejecting shot evolved into a spectacular hole-in-one. We all celebrated the wonder together. All of a sudden, we were chatty and felt lifted, and we all shared in the energy of this player's good fortune. We were rejuvenated by his experience.

At the time, I just enjoyed the moment and didn't give much thought to the lesson that that round of golf had taught me. Since I started playing golf with Geshe-la, though, I've learned to pay attention to and enjoy the successes of the other players in my group. I celebrate the good shots with them and encourage them through the poor ones. I enjoy sharing my creative shot visualizations with them, even when the actual shot didn't quite turn out the way I intended. It creates exciting conversation and camaraderie around the game that has brought us together. This has rewarded me with rejuvenation of spirit and mind. I've realized how my old way of playing within my closed energy box of self-focus made the game I love seem more like work. I've broken free from that, and I now find I'm revitalized by sharing in the energy of the game with those with me. Sharing my love and excitement of the game and enjoying others' experiences along the way is fulfilling. It fills my cup, so to speak.

Some golfers really enjoy the walk and the opportunity to be outside enjoying the elements as well as the people. If this is how you get rejuvenated with fresh energy, then acknowledge that and have that be your intention when you go to play golf. Don't let others get you trapped in worrying about the score; avoid getting attached to the results and maybe don't even keep score. Be aware of bringing your attention back to your intention, which was to take in the trees, the fresh air, the deer, and the people that may have joined you.

See if you can break down the game into one shot at a time, as its own creative task that you get to manifest any way you want to, each time you swing. You might feel energized by each opportunity as it comes along. You will get to create something out of nothing, or even something great out of difficult circumstances, every time you stand over the ball. I notice people can do this on the driving range, as each shot stands alone and is not attached to score. When they play golf, though, their heavy focus on the score takes away from the enjoyment of each individual shot. I encourage you to think about that the next time you play, even if it is a competitive round.

Rejuvenating our energy through an activity is about feeling better after the activity than before we started it. If you play golf to rejuvenate your spirit and energy, be aware of what you enjoy about it. What elements of the game make you feel good when you play golf? Focusing on score and improving score can be a positive goal to have, but don't forget to find and focus on the elements that fill you with joy in the journey of the game.

At the end of the round, it's important to recognize the positive energy that you gained, so that you can put a lid on your full cup, so to speak, and feel satisfied as you leave. This way you focus on the fulfillment, and the rejuvenation continues even after your round, when you get to recount the day and share your stories with others.

Reflection

Can you think back on a round of golf where your energy or that of the group changed for the better? My story of the lucky hole-in-one will always remind me of how rejuvenating it is to let our energies flow. Energy is abundant and is contagious when shared.

Enjoy the creation process of every shot. And try sharing those intentions, successes, or failures with others. It may fill your rejuvenation cup as it does for me.

20. Confidence

It does not matter if people think you are
good or not
It does not matter what you think
It only matters what you feel for yourself
in your heart
The *only* matter is to know yourself
and trust yourself
Walk with confidence
Speak with confidence
Listen with confidence
Sit with confidence
Look with confidence
Work with confidence
Stand with confidence
Swing with confidence
Always being confident

—Geshe-la

Geshe-la

IN MY LIFE, I have learned about confidence in two different ways.

First, I learned how important it is for a child to have a foundation of confidence provided by their parents or caregivers. Role models who provide unconditional love, care, and guidance provide children with a strong base of confidence they will carry through their lives.

I have a large family with many cousins. I've noticed that children who grow up with loving and nurturing parents become more confident people. And I've noticed that some of my other cousins who were sent away to be educated in India have a lower confidence level. My observation is that it is very important to grow up with your own loving parents. The children feel that love even if the rest of the world is against them. It makes a big difference in their confidence level.

For myself, I didn't have much confidence as a child. I didn't grow up with my parents; I was raised by aunties and uncles and other family members. When I went to the monastery, I was fortunate to be taught by Venerable Master Wako Gyaltsen. I lived with him and he became like a father figure to me. He taught me from ages thirteen to eighteen. My confidence grew when I lived with him: I knew he would protect me and I bloomed under his love and kindness. Living in an environment that provides care, guidance, and love is the first way to develop confidence.

The second way to develop confidence is through spiritual and psychological practice. You can learn who you truly are through the spiritual teachings. I have learned so much about myself over twenty years through meditation. I know who I am and how I treat people.

I've also learned through teaching others. I know that I teach well when I am truly connected to who I am. My authentic self connects through the teachings and gives me a profound sense of confidence. I accept myself without approval of others and I feel good in myself. But if I depend on the approval of others and they withhold it, then my confidence is gone. I have given my power to them.

Today I feel at peace and am grateful to know who I truly am. I feel as comfortable and confident meeting new people as I do with old friends. When I visit relatives from Washington, DC, and in California, they also see my confidence. They say even my laughter is deeper and more self-assured.

Thus, confidence can be built in childhood through loving guidance. You can also build it yourself by connecting to your authentic self. It will help you in everything you do, both on and off the course.

There are also two things we need to cultivate to be confident. One is to know who you are, and the other is to know what you're doing.

What does it mean, to know who you are? There is a moment when you feel at peace. There is a feeling of fullness and contentment. You are aware of your actions and your intentions. You are aware of the words you are using. And you are very comfortable and at peace with them. This is to fully know yourself with confidence. You do not have to depend on others for proof of who you are, but you can feel the comfort of connection to who you are from the inside.

Often when we don't know our true self, we depend on others' approval or opinions or perceptions of us. When somebody says, "Oh, you are wonderful," you feel, "Oh, I'm wonderful!" When someone says you're terrible, then you feel you're terrible. You're allowing a person's opinion of you in that moment to define you. When we're always looking for someone else to tell us who we are or to accept us, then we have no confidence in who we are, as it changes all the time.

When you know who you are, it doesn't matter what somebody else says. If somebody says you're wonderful, it doesn't make you feel "up," and if someone says you're terrible, it doesn't make you feel "down." You know yourself. You're aware of who you are and your behavior. You're at peace and clear about your intentions and actions. When you reach that state of stillness, then that's it—you know yourself, and you are confident. That clarity of you knowing yourself is one aspect of confidence.

The other aspect of confidence we need to cultivate is to know what we're doing. This comes from deep wisdom—deep wisdom and knowledge that come with study and practice. If you know, really know, how to do something, you feel confident. In golf, for example, you need to know how to hit the ball, what to hit it with, where to go, etc. You need to find this information, put it into practice, and become proficient at it. You know what you've studied and practiced. You're confident that you'll hit the ball. You know how to hit, what to hit with, how to swing, the speed of swing, and all the information that helps you play the game. When you have the knowledge and the wisdom of the swing, of golfing, and you have consistently practiced, then you will have confidence.

This applies to anything you do, not just golf. When you know, you have confidence. When you don't know, you don't have confidence. Confidence comes from knowing who you are and also knowing what to do. Those are the two key points. Many people have no confidence because they're lacking one or the other. They are unsure and nervous.

Know yourself and know what you're doing.

Reflection

What does confidence mean to you?

Many people are confident in some situations but not others. Do you see yourself as a confident person? If not, how will you develop the confidence you need?

How do you approach each club? Is the grip and swing the same, or do you approach each one differently? I find I have special connections to each club; some are easy to hit, but others are much harder for me. I know it's not the club but my own connection and confidence.

Jesse

CONFIDENCE COMES from learning and practicing skills or habits. When we practice a learned skill, like memorizing writing, singing, or playing a sport, we're able to do the task without too much work, and there's a calming sense of knowing that we'll be successful. Your confidence in what you practice will continue to grow as your skill level improves and you learn more tools to achieve your goal. In the game of golf, whether you're a player that shoots under par regularly or one just starting out, there will be certain aspects of your game that you feel more comfortable with. Every player knows that they need to work on the weaker parts of their game, for example, bunker shots, and through doing so they're able to gain knowledge and practice that skill in order to bring more confidence to their game as a whole.

A friend and great teacher of mine, Charlie King, an esteemed member of the PGA of America, helped me learn to build confidence in a weaker skill in my game. I was playing in a tournament, and he came driving around in a golf cart to watch his students that were playing. He asked me how I was doing. I said, "Charlie, I just can't draw the ball out here. I can do it on the driving range, but I just can't do it out here on the course."

I had played golf with a natural fade to the right since I started playing golf and Charlie had been teaching me how to control ball flight and to hit a draw when I needed to. He wanted me to develop these skills so that I felt confident hitting any shot I might need on the course. I had been working hard to produce a draw shot on the driving range, but my lack of confidence to produce a right-to-left shot shape on the course was on display. I just wouldn't trust the knowledge and practice I had gained to allow myself to use it on the golf course.

Charlie looked at me and said, "Jesse, just start with one. Just do one." At that point I was overwhelmed with trying to control my score and scared to try something new, but when he said, "Just do one," it made it seem possible, more digestible, and not so scary. Just hit one shot with commitment and see what happens. It seemed crazy to fear that. On the next hole, I faced a shot that would benefit from a right-to-left draw, and I buckled down to do it. Just one! I had a three-fairway wood in my hand for a drive on a par 4 dogleg left, and a draw would shape the shot perfectly down the curving fairway. Midway through my swing I hesitated in trusting my swing and didn't get my weight off my back foot soon enough. The hesitant leg movement, along with the full-draw release of the clubhead, sent my ball with a sweeping draw too far to the left, and as I feared it would, it jumped out of bounds. I remember feeling the pent-up stress in my body after I hit it, but I smiled and I thought, "I did it. I hit the ball with a draw." I made a double bogey on that hole, but that one attempt opened the floodgates, as I produced the shape I wanted. I just needed to commit and have more faith. I tried again on a later hole, and again it wasn't a perfect shot, but it was a draw and was in the fairway. From that day on, every time I tried that particular shot, I got better, and as I saw improvements, I became a believer and my confidence grew. Now I love to shape golf shots. In fact, I find it harder to hit a straight shot. I love to create my shots like I'm painting my round of golf, and I thank Charlie for opening that door for me.

I have lots of students who've worked hard on the driving range making swing improvements and then are unable to transfer them to the course due to lack of confidence. When a player goes to the course, their focus turns to the score, and they try to control their swing in order to not make an error. It's like they want to hold on to the steering wheel too tight for fear of going off course. It's difficult to give up control and try something new, but remember the advice from my great teacher: "Just do it once." It's a great place to start.

So what if it isn't perfect the first time? We all make errors on the golf course anyway, so why not give one shot a try. Then you can try it again and again. One shot at a time. Changing your approach to a whole round of golf can seem overwhelming and scary, but to try something once is easy and not that costly for a whole round of golf. Even if you only try once in the round and then go back to the practice range again, that one effort will open the door to believing in yourself and turning down the fear. We all know the proverb "How do you eat an elephant? One bite at a time."

People do often have a hard time if they improve their swing once but then make a mistake on the second or third time. They're afraid of failure and return to what they're comfortable with, even if the result isn't great, as their old way is familiar and more predictable. They give up on themselves quickly and have no confidence in the new skill they've been practicing. This fear prevents them from achieving their goal of improving their skill.

If you feel like one of these players, see if you can commit yourself to executing the new method of a shot just once a round, followed by more practice. Confidence in a new or improved skill must be practiced on the golf course to own it, and the rewards are tremendous. I love to go out on the course in the evenings when it's quieter and play nine holes just to practice new skills on the course. I don't focus on score at all but rather on trying my practiced skill without fear, so that I can build a memory bank of positive shots that increases my confidence and rewards me with fun and achievement. When you learn to use a new skill on the course one swing at a time, you own it, you master it, and you can apply it with more confidence every time. It's a great way to add more skills to your golfing toolbox, which will in turn give you more confidence in your whole game as it becomes more developed all the way around.

One interesting aspect of golf that challenges your confidence level is the changing elements. The weather changes day to day, and different courses have different layouts and visuals. When I've taken even a good player to a different golf course to play a tournament with me, their confidence dwindles because things look different. There's an element of the unknown that rattles the confidence. When I go to other courses to play, I remember something my wife shared with me: "A shot is a shot is a shot, no matter what's between you and the hole." She meant that you decide on the shot you want to hit and execute the swing you've practiced on the range or on any other golf course. It doesn't matter if there's an out-of-bounds on the left, or a hazard on the right, or a dogleg to fly over; it's the same swing you practiced and the same ball flight you've seen a thousand times before. Commit to what you know; the layout in front of you is just a visual distraction.

Sometimes, the layout of a particular course may suit you more than another, depending on the natural or grooved tendencies of your swing. Some courses require fade shots, some draws to the left, and some a high trajectory in order to score well. It's good to recognize that you'll feel more comfortable on some layouts than on others, and when competing to score well, it's always good to play what's called the percentage shot—the shot you're the most confident in at that moment. This is because you're more confident in the outcome and can plan the hole accordingly. You'll notice that on the PGA Tour even the best have certain layouts that they play better on. Confidence comes from knowing your strengths, using them regularly, and practicing new skills to add to your bag of tricks at least once a round, so that they become familiar, and you own them as yours when you need them.

I get to hear lots of golf talk at the club and there's a mix of positive and negative stories all the time. There are those that boast out loud about their great shots and feel full of ego-driven confidence at the end of the day, and then there are the stories of self-destruction from those who feel defeated. Rather than riding this rollercoaster of good and bad experiences, try to cultivate a quiet confidence, one based not on ego but on knowing that you have good information, are working at applying it every day, and are focused on that process. There is a steadiness and peace to this confidence that does not care about what others think. Being comfortable with yourself and the path you're on is confidence, and it allows you to grow it a little every day.

I'm grateful to Charlie for teaching me to start with one and let the confidence grow from there. When you are learning something new, doing it just once on the golf course gives you the knowledge that you have the ability to do it again. From that building block you just let the confidence build, one shot at a time.

Reflection

Do you ever wake up feeling overwhelmed by the day ahead?

I've also applied "just do one" to my daily life. I've evolved the idea a little; I focus on living ten minutes at a time, and in that way move through the day or the situation one moment at a time. It helps me take small bites out of any situation, and I feel my confidence and peace grow as I work my way through the day. At the end of a tough day, I feel stronger, more capable, and more confident in myself.

Try this in a round of golf if you are stressed about playing with new people. Or try it in your daily life. Build your confidence with knowledge and then "just do one."

21. Conclusion

Geshe-la

GOLF IS a unique sport. It allows us to walk in a beautiful environment for a few hours and improve both our physical and psychological health. In this game you can exercise your focus, your ability to let go, and your compassion for yourself and others. Spiritually, I make a powerful connection with the elements of space, air, fire, water, and earth while I play. I know that I must attend to my mental state, or the game will become very difficult, and I appreciate that I can improve my well-being through golf. The skills needed to play golf are the same needed to manage work and home life.

Golf can teach you a great deal about yourself and your life. It's not just hitting a ball; your swing and how you strike the ball can be an example of your life's journey. To hit the ball well, you must handle your emotions and it's good for your heart to be open. It's important to integrate these skills in the rest of your life.

Golf has been an excellent commitment for me. I know what I need to accomplish before playing. I know that discipline and focus will provide me with a substantial sense of accomplishment. Golf brings tremendous reward to my life.

Golf remains a mystery to me, a mystery that compels me to return to the course time and time again to learn something new, both about myself and the game. Golf is wonderful because it gives immediate feedback as to where my mind is at and how I'm doing. Gripping the club too tightly or worrying about my last shot will provide immediate feedback that I've lost my focus, and my swing will be off, and my ball will not land where I expected. But if I can hold the space and be balanced in stillness, my swing will be effortless and my ball more cooperative. It's all in the head.

Recently I decided to play a round of golf even though it was raining steadily. By the tenth hole I was playing at 1 over par and feeling confident that I would finish strong despite the rain. I was so confident that I took a video of myself at 1 over and sent it to golf buddies so they could also enjoy my splendid play. But something shifted. The next holes were mostly bogeys or double bogeys. I was no longer balanced. My ego was in charge and had big expectations that I would do well. But the mystery of golf and the lessons of the course that day told me that I should have stayed focused in the present moment. It was better to be a nobody out enjoying the game than be "a good golfer." As I realized what had happened to me, I knew I was no longer present in the game because my feelings and intentions were more attached to the video and my friends' impressions of me. Expectations create obstacles and can destroy you. Being focused in the present moment and letting go of other thoughts holds the space of clear awareness and the game becomes much easier.

I acknowledged the shift in me and recognized that I felt tight. Fear of failure had built up in me. I worked to let go of my expectations. I thought if I could hit one good shot, I would accept that as success. Half good shots and half bad shots would be fine. I let go of pars and birdies and did my best to consciously shift my energy. While playing, sometimes I sing like I did when I was a boy working alone as a shepherd in the Himalayas. This can create a new, relaxing space around me and allow me to focus on the game.

That day still ended with less success than usual, but it caused me to reflect on how golf always gives you immediate feedback on your mental state. Paying attention to this feedback is accepting a great gift.

I've seen some people try to compensate for a lack of mental focus with new clubs, a new course, or new playing partners. All of these may be helpful, but it is my experience that by working on my focus and mental ability, I'll have a much more enjoyable game.

Accepting that every game of golf will provide new challenges will help us be gentle with ourselves. Lacking this quality of gentleness can destroy ourselves, our game, and our friendships. Learning to be gentle with ourselves as we confront obstacles is a great gift. Being kind with ourselves and others is a great way to feel at peace.

I think that every golfer has their own secret techniques that reflect their own journey of what works best for them. It's secret and just for them and occurs when they're balanced and focused. I hope that the reader will find techniques in this book that will work well for them and become a part of their game and life.

I've found that the game of golf helps me deal with everyday life when I'm aware that I am surrounded by the beauty of the elements and that this is not just a walk on the golf course. Golf reminds us of who we are and what we're supposed to do. The true master can master their swing, their emotions, and everything around them. Approaching the game with a relaxed attitude, slowing down, managing your expectations, focusing, and having confidence will help you find your true master. Confidence and commitment are crucial in every shot and in life. Golf is a mirror reflecting the self. Becoming a master is learning how to handle your emotions and how to connect to nature and the people around you. When you find this, you're not just wasting your time hitting balls.

Jesse

WRITING THIS BOOK with Geshe-la has been a precious and introspective journey for me. It has given me time to reminisce, reflect, and gather the experience and growth opportunities that golf has gifted me.

I have always loved golf and the challenge of learning to play it well. At first golf was a safe and wholesome activity that my mom left my brother and me to do as teenagers after school. It quickly grew to a passion, an obsession, and a career. I have loved every minute of studying the mechanics of the golf swing and the nuances of successful players of the game. It has nurtured relationships where I have been both student and teacher—often at the same time. I have realized that we learn and teach in many personal encounters every day, and so I listen to and value those around me.

When I started out as a young student of the game, I sought guidance from teachers to learn the fundamentals—walking, talking, and mirroring those around me, like a child learning the basic skills of life. The more I learned, the more questions I asked and the deeper I looked at myself and the knowledge around me. I connected with masters of the game at different levels, and they all assisted in my development. As I grew, I started to develop my own interpretation of the golf swing, my own ideas of how to best assist others to improve, and my own ways to communicate my understanding of this wonderous game.

I worked hard at improving my game, searching for masters of the swing to guide me. As I grew as an adult, husband, and father, I started to realize the potential for mental and spiritual growth in my game and in life. The more I discussed the mental aspects of golf, the clearer my awareness of myself as a person became. It is funny how having children and paying attention to how they develop, seeing their need for loving patience and guidance, mirrors the need to continue to offer that to yourself. I started to see the world so differently and had an appreciation for the beauty of the universe and its possibilities around me.

Then I met Geshe-la, the master who is showing me how to keep developing the master within myself. Once we are adults, we have learned enough about life to be independent, but it is a gift of life to keep nurturing our learning and connection to the universe to be the best version of ourselves that we can be. We can all be our own master of life, of golf, and of any activity we choose to put time and effort into. Golf offers an amazing journey of inner growth and self-realization, because in playing you share space with the great outdoors, time with fellow golfers, and time to walk and talk with yourself. It offers the challenge and opportunity to get to know yourself really well and requires focus and kindness to yourself to enjoy the process.

I always say to my son that the one lesson I have learned from this great game is that the only person you need to conquer in this world is yourself, and when you learn to be your own master, everything is glorious. It is a continuous journey but one worth living. May you enjoy your continued journey to finding your master on the golf course and in life.

Acknowledgments

Geshe-la

First, I acknowledge all my masters and spiritual teachers, some of whom have passed on and some of whom are still alive. I am very grateful for their blessings.

I am grateful to all the friends I play golf with. During my first twenty years of playing golf, I never took lessons; I just learned from my friends. These wonderful people shared tips and advice that allowed me to learn this amazing game. The first lessons I ever took were from Jesse and Nadine, and I thank them for teaching me.

I am grateful for the effort and kindness of my student Esther Hutton. She helped to transcribe this book. I am also grateful to Jennifer Walton, my longtime friend and student, who golfed with me at the beginning and helped edit this book.

My gratitude goes also to my friends and students Harvey Rice and Jackie Cole. I am so appreciative of their professional editing prowess.

Finally, I thank Amala for all she did to support me. I am grateful as well for Anne Marie Hartman and her kindness and support. My appreciation and gratitude also go to Norma Chambers for all of her time and effort in organizing my teaching schedule so that I can enjoy more time on the golf course.

Jesse

I WOULD LIKE to thank the following people for the ways they have supported my growth and the adventures that have inspired me to write this book with Geshe-la.

Nadine Ash, my wife: for all the support in the world, through all my faults, failures, and triumphs. Within seven days of knowing you, I knew you were the one for me.

Geshe-la: for supporting my ideas of golf and life, and for believing in my ability to teach you how to bring golf to the forefront of the fulfillment you feel in life.

Harvey Rice and Jackie Cole: I am so appreciative of the great day at the golf course we shared and of your editing touches.

Esther Hutton and Jennifer Walton: for helping us collaborate our ideas and organize the thoughts and lessons we wanted to share in this book.

Satuot Moussa, my mom: for your support and love when direction and purpose were nowhere to be found in my life.

Javan Moussa, my son: for teaching me to be myself and to trust the many facets that make me "me."

About the Authors

Geshe YongDong Losar

Geshe YongDong Losar (Geshe-la) is a Buddhist master originally from Tibet. He lives in Courtenay, British Columbia, where he established and directs Sherab Chamma Ling, the only Tibetan Bon Buddhist center in Canada. He teaches in many centers and universities around the world and has also founded the Bon Da Ling center in Costa Rica.

Geshe YongDong was born in 1969 in northeastern Tibet. As a boy, his desire to become a monk was intensified by the death of his mother, the death of his grandmother, and the three years he spent alone in the harsh Himalayan mountains tending a flock of over six hundred sheep for his uncle. At the age of thirteen, he entered a monastery.

Eleven years later, after completing specialized training, he was awarded the *geshe* degree, an academic achievement of the highest order, similar to a Western doctorate in theology. He escaped Tibet soon after, settling in India, before relocating to Canada.

In 2022 Wisdom Publications published Geshe-la's book *Calm Breath, Calm Mind: A Guide to the Healing Power of Breath.*

Jesse Moussa

Jesse has extensive education in golf management and instruction in Canada and the United States and has been a Class A Professional with the CPGA since 2007. He developed his career from an apprentice with the CPGA, to a Class A member, and has continued his commitment to the game and the industry for more than twenty years. His passion is in growing the love of the game and developing ways to make teaching more effective and learning more fun. Jesse is an inventor of a patented golf training aid, the Right Touch, which he developed to help his students wipe out the stubborn slice, with the backing of world-renowned instructors Fred Griffin and Mike Adams. His passion lies in inspiring confidence, enjoyment, and progress in his students and fellow instructors. He believes that improving your skills can be as much fun as playing the game. Jesse's favorite place to be, other than home, is at the golf course, sharing his love of the game while supporting others, and playing and honing his own skills, too.

Explore More with Wisdom Publications

Listen to Geshela on the Wisdom Podcast, watch his Dharma Chat, enroll in his online course, or read his other book, *Calm Breath, Calm Mind: A Guide to the Healing Power of Breath*:

"[*Calm Breath, Calm Mind* is] a deep and didactic exploration into the ancient art of Bön breathing from a master of the form. Highly recommended." —James Nestor, *New York Times* bestselling author of *Breath: The New Science of a Lost Art*

Investigate Widely with These Authors

Mindfulness in Plain English: 20th Anniversary Edition
Bhante Gunaratana

"A classic—one of the very best English sources for authoritative explanations of mindfulness."—Daniel Goleman, author of *Emotional Intelligence*

Meditation for Modern Madness
His Eminence the Seventh Dzogchen Rinpoche

"This book by His Eminence Dzogchen Rinpoche is offered in the manner of a gift for the entire Dzogchen lineage and is a must-read for Buddhists in general and for Buddhist scholars whose motivation, minds, and goals are vast."—from the foreword by His Eminence Alak Zenkar Rinpoche

About Wisdom Publications

Wisdom Publications is the leading publisher of classic and contemporary Buddhist books and practical works on mindfulness. To learn more about us or to explore our other books, please visit our website at wisdom.org or contact us at the address below.

Wisdom Publications
132 Perry Street
New York, NY 10014 USA

We are a 501(c)(3) organization, and donations in support of our mission are tax deductible.

Wisdom Publications is affiliated with the Foundation for the Preservation of the Mahayana Tradition (FPMT).